ADVANCE PRAISE FOR *The Healer's Way*

"I didn't want to put this book down! Earnie Larsen is validating and inspirational as he speaks about the heart and soul of recovery and healing from the consequences of love denied. He captures the reader with heartfelt stories, wonderful phraseology, and great analogies. As both an educator and an author he personally embodies and describes the depth of spirit that makes change possible."

> —Claudia Black, Ph.D., author of *It Will Never Happen To Me*

"Larsen is a genius. No living counselor and author brings more wisdom on healing or more walk to their talk. I applied Larsen's *The Healer's Way* seven-step process and it was key in healing me physically, emotionally, and spiritually, not to mention financially."

> —Tom Gegax, author of *The Big Book of Small Business*

"*The Healer's Way* guides the millions of us who are broken and explains what has happened, and now what to do. It puts words to, and makes sense of, a journey that sometimes gets very difficult. It is always changing, and the work never ends. The good news is that there is great JOY! ahead . . . and Earnie Larsen continues to light the way for anyone seeking it."

> —John McAndrew, songwriter/singer

"Once again, Earnie has captured the essence of our humanness. A master storyteller and communicator, his *The Healer's Way* speaks to our need for connection, balance, and healing, and provides a glimpse into God's ultimate gift to each of us . . . love; and is a great reminder of what our primary purpose truly is . . ."

> —Mike Neatherton, Executive Vice President and COO, Betty Ford Center

"I have been an Earnie Larsen fan for almost thirty years now. While he is known for his seminars and many books, what is less known about him is the hundreds of people that he has helped and has personally changed their lives. This book is a gathering of those peoples' stories, a delightful gathering at a dance called grace. Listen carefully to this insightful gem of collected stories of how God participates in the dances of the common folk. Earnie has a way of helping each of us to see the Lord of the Dance in our lives."

> —The Rev. Dr. Jo Campe, Pastor of "The Recovery Churches" in Minnesota

"The best of healers always seem to possess some magic gifts for helping others, but it is rare that these gifts are shared with other healers. This book is an exception. It teaches and touches at the same time. Earnie and Carol are to be commended for a great contribution to the art of healing. Their book is full of rich stories that always reflect that the core of healing is spirituality. I thank them for reminding us of this."

> —Robert J. Ackerman, Ph.D., Professor and Director of the Mid-Atlantic Addiction Training Center

the
Healer's way

the
Healer's way

*Bringing Hands-On Compassion
to a Love-Starved World*

EARNIE LARSEN
with CAROL LARSEN HEGARTY

Conari Press

To Battle Angels everywhere
especially those who showed up for us.

First published in 2007 by Conari Press,
an imprint of Red Wheel/Weiser, LLC
With offices at:
500 Third Street, Suite 230
San Francisco, CA 94107
www.redwheelweiser.com

ISBN-10: 1-57324-309-4
ISBN-13: 978-1-57324-309-4

Library of Congress Cataloging-in-Publication Data
Larsen, Earnest.
The Healers way: bringing hands-on compassion to a love-starved world /
Earnie Larsen and Carol Larsen Hegarty.
        p. cm.
ISBN-13: 978-1-57324-309-4 (alk. paper)
ISBN-10: 1-57324-309-4 (alk. paper)
1. Compassion. 2. Compassion–Religious aspects. 3. Healing. I.
Hegarty, Carol. II. Title.

BJ1475.L37 2007
241'.4–dc22

2007010924

Cover and interior design by Maija Tollefson
Typeset in Minion
Cover photograph Bobby Model © Getty images

Printed in the United States
TS
10   9   8   7   6   5   4   3   2   1

 Text paper contains a minimum of 50% post-consumer-waste material.

contents

The Healer's Way

The idea for this book was born in one of those sacramental moments when time stands still and the routine paths of daily life give way to an unexpected door leading to a deeper level. Such fabled moments are said to occur in the context of transcendent experiences, such as the birth of a child or the death of a loved one. Yet the world is full of surprises, isn't it? Sometimes these invitations to the "beyond" arise totally unexpectedly from seemingly ordinary-as-dirt events. God's tap on the shoulder can happen anytime. One of my sacramental moments was when Kurt simply asked for my help.

At that time Kurt was maybe twenty-five. He had finished four hard years of college and laid claim to what many of his generation seem to regard as their inalienable right, if not duty—a year of bumming around Europe with a backpack and a list of youth hostels.

Kurt was traveling when his soul caught fire. In striking clarity, he realized that he wanted to be a healer, to make a positive difference in this hurting and hurtful world. He wanted his life to count. Why *then*? Who knows, but the brick wall of his previous consciousness had suddenly given way to a golden door.

Souls don't need to travel to Europe to catch fire, of course. Angels with matches are everywhere, and for some reason, they seem to love youth best. Kurt just happened to be in Europe when the flame caught him.

So, fired up with that special enthusiasm known only to youth (and too often left there), Kurt returned to the United States like a marine assaulting a beachhead. Laying claim to his education, he took a job at a social-service agency. Before long that agency sent him to a conference on post-traumatic stress syndrome. That's where I met him.

I had been going to similar conferences for thirty years. How those decades passed so quickly, I have no idea; they just did. One morning I woke up and thirty years had disappeared! On the day I met Kurt no small part of me saw my youthful self in him. "I know you!" I said to myself. "You're the kid who went to a conference like this one thirty years ago. You feel righteous indignation at the state of the world, don't you? You have absolute certainty that you (meaning people your age) can and will create a brave new world. With all your heart you believe that you can improve anything that had ever gone before."

Beyond that, however—way beyond, at least for this man-child of so long ago—was the desire to learn. I wanted to find a teacher. To get next to someone who had gone before, had earned some wisdom, and had not sold out or dropped out. Someone who had hung in there long enough to have something important to pass along: the Secret. Surely, behind all the hustle and bustle, all the noise and commotion, was a secret—you know, the core, the heart of the matter. There had to be a pure and simple truth that lit up the way ahead. Surely there must be someone a newcomer could walk with, learn from, be protected by when necessary, until he or she could navigate the rough terrain alone.

After that original conference, Kurt and I frequently met to talk. We discussed client situations, how to deal with the ever-present irritation of office politics, and dozens of other topics from the philosophical to the practical. Then one day Kurt asked me if I would more formally teach him what I had learned over the years. For me, that moment was sacramental and precious indeed.

My walk was winding down, his just starting. More often than not, when the bell rings I just sit there wondering where all the fire went. Yet it was still unthinkable that the work not continue. Kurt was asking—though he didn't know it, not yet—if he could be my replacement. In him was the mirror that perhaps I was to someone who went before me, reflecting both backward and out through the ages. The moment made me think of John McCrae's poem from World War I:

Take up our quarrel with the foe
to you from failing hands we throw
the torch; be yours to hold it high. . . .

So began our walk. Over the next few years I committed myself to plumbing the depths of a lifetime's experiences, conversations, journals, poems, letters, tapes—every resource that I'd drawn on, I pressed down to squeeze out the sticky, pure essence of whatever it was the years had done to and given me—what I had learned from the Dance of Healing.

I hope it will be helpful to Kurt—and to you, dear reader. Some of you are probably involved in ministry or serve as parole officers, social workers, or health-care professionals. I know that these days school teachers are called upon to do double duty as social workers and communicators of traditional life lessons. Others without number are also healing caregivers—not by profession, but by inclination. Are you one who provides support for those suffering from AIDS or other terminal illnesses? Do you befriend the lonely elderly or serve neglected children in some way? Perhaps some readers are members of a twelve-step program of recovery or are parents of children who have lost their way.

There are plenty of people who understand, in fear and trembling, that "we make society and then society makes us," to paraphrase Henry David Thoreau. What is being made all around us is an environment increasingly hostile to the human spirit. You, dear reader, can change that environment. The pale horse of the Apocalypse is among us in many forms. Do you dare to cast your lot with Kurt? Healers are simply those whose vision dictates that they face the dreaded horseman saying, "Not here. Not now. In my space today you may not enter."

These pages that I prepared for Kurt are about one thing and one thing only: the spiritual alchemy involved in the amazing-grace process of personal transformation.

By definition, healing is about change. Why do people change? How do they change? I've focused on those potent moments, the culmination of incredible movements of energy, whether we recognize them or not, at which we become able to see another, higher path—and take it. That is what healing is, whether it wears the face of acceptance or forgiveness, whether it is about totally changing the direction of one's life or simply opening up to life's deeper meaning (which isn't a simple task at all). Perhaps it's summoning the courage to stand up again after being knocked down so hard you think you'll never be able get up.

How does healing happen and how can the process of healing best be aided? Is it in fact even *possible* to leave the world better than we found it?

Perhaps this communication to young Kurt will be of some benefit to others like you, dear reader, who are determined to make a difference. Such would be the fondest wish of my generation's foot soldiers on the path of healing. To you we pass the torch.

chapter 1

The Secret

WHAT AM I DOING UP AT 2:30 IN THE MORNING?!

Whenever I am emotionally at war over something, I slam awake, always about this same hour. Once awake, I might as well get up and do something because I'm sure as heck not getting back to sleep.

So what is it this time?

To tell the truth, I've been dragging my feet over starting this set of pages for weeks. Why am I hesitating? What I feel is mostly fear—fear and an overwhelming sense of incompetence. There's nothing I want more than to communicate truth to you, at least truth as I have experienced it. That was all Kurt asked of me. The trouble is that *this* truth—dealing with the human condition, healing the human spirit—is infinitely greater than I, or than all of us put together. We human beings are just tiny twigs sweeping by in the River of Life. The River, of course, is eternal; we are but momentary. As I sit here in my chilly little home office, sur-rounded by memories swirling out of the darkness, even think-ing of capturing these truths in words seems a hopeless cause at best, an insult at worst. In a way, it's a crown of thorns to the heart.

Not that all of life is so painful. It is not. Your involvement with the human condition may thrust you into the depths of hell, but it will also lift you so high your wings will brush the very face of God! Perhaps you will find, as I have, that too much beauty can also bruise the heart. That's the point—the big picture is just too much for us. Our pockets are so small, the treasure so vast!

I feel like a character in one of those delightfully mysterious scenes from a Disney movie. The wrinkled old shaman pulls some magical powders from his pouch and throws it into the fire. Fantastic forms immediately arise out of the smoke, visions of what was or will be, perhaps hidden in memories no longer retrievable except through the shaman's magic. Having opened the door to the world beyond, the old shaman patiently sits there, watching the shadows dance on the walls of his cave.

I've often reflected that each of us lives in the cave of personal existence, fashioned from what we have drawn from our experiences. I envision that the cave has a door that gives access to the magic within. We need only enter to tap into the mysteries. So I urge you to open the door and wait. Be patient. Like the old shaman, throw your magic grains on the fire and then sit back and greet whatever responds to your invitation. Even if it scares you, it will be the truth, the beckoning light you must follow to find your way—wherever it leads. The path my well surprise you. However well you think you know your destination, the light will invariably lead you elsewhere, perhaps to a strange place you never knew existed. Just summon the courage to greet whatever comes through the door.

I sit here at my old typewriter on this dark, early morning and cast my herbs on the fire. The shadows are dancing. I hear murmuring all through the cave. So many faces begin to materialize! They all want to talk to you, my friend. They want your ear—and your heart and soul. They would carry you off. Not away into their world, but more deeply into your own. That is where the journey always leads—down, down, down into your own depths. You can reach out as healer only to the extent that you are willing to reach in. It's about essence, my friend, always essence before action. Actions can lie nearly as well as words, but essence speaks only the truth. So many are here, asking for you. . . .

Yet I know I must be careful. All these dear people who would speak to you are my most prized possessions. I feel like a goofy grandparent (and I am one) who at the drop of a hat produces dozens of pictures of his grandkids with no explanation other than "I love them." I could fill a thousand pages with stories—great stories that deserve to be told—but I don't want to do that. I'd rather stitch just some of the stories into a pattern. No matter how pointedly storytellers tell their tales, however, I realize that listeners always take away what they will.

But I am on a mission, and *I want to lead you in a specific direction.* As best I can, I want these stories to serve as reference points, as examples of the pattern I will explain. That is what Kurt asked for—on your behalf, for all I know—and that is what I will do my best to give you.

Once you hear what I have to say, we will meet and talk. At that time you may well say, "I heard you, but I do not agree. It is not as I have experienced it." *Great!* Then we will get up on the table and dance! What truth has the healing way revealed to *you?* When you tell me, we will both be richer. But for the time being, please listen with your heart as well as your ears. Try on what I—and my friends—share with you, as you would a warm coat on a winter evening. Wear it. Merge it with your experiences as you walk more deeply into our world. Try it out first. Then we will talk.

A last word about goofy grandparents. I thought this was funny. A friend of mine once said, "You think your grandkids poop ice cream." Probably true. In much the same way, I believe that the people you will meet in these stories poop ice cream. Each one of these people and their stories is precious to me. (Doesn't every one of us need a few people around who think we poop ice cream?)

It's best if you read these pages deliberately, for this isn't a novel or trainer's manual. The people I'm presenting to you are willing to share their secrets because *they seek a relationship with you*, and as with all relationships, it takes time—time and respect—for the parties to get to know one another. I have no idea what they will tell you. That is between you and the keeper of your soul. Whatever their message, you may not hear it until you visit them a second or third time. So often we hurry right past unrecognized diamonds! But if you make a friend of silence and grow accustomed to waiting before your open door, rest assured that you will learn to listen to your own messengers, who will surround you in dizzying abundance. As you listen and learn, what they say will become who you are. Then, one marvelous day, it will be your turn. You will recognize your soul in the fresh face of another who will ask you, as Kurt asked me, to walk side by side through the shadows. It is a good thing to go in company, for the healing way, though grounded in beauty, is difficult and dangerous.

So on we go.

Here are snapshots of two different times, two different places.

A. I found this in a journal from 1969: "I can't heal you, I can't heal myself. My own weakness is thundering so loudly, I can't hear you at all. I'm lost. I don't know what to do."

I don't recall what that was about, but it sounds like hard times, doesn't it? The first four words were right enough—I *can't* heal anyone else. Even the thought of assuming that kind of responsibility is enough to make the strongest would-be healer run for the hills. God save us from those who assume responsibility for others' outcomes!

B. This one is from June 4, 1994:

I might be lost, God,
but
you aren't.
It is sufficient.

Getting from A to B took me only twenty-five years. And even now I don't stay put in B very well.

※

Have you heard this story? A man was drowning. A counselor rowed out to him. The man said, "Oh, good, you are here to save me!" The counselor replied, "No, I'm not. I'm here to teach you to swim." Pretty good, huh?

※

What seems like a thousand years ago, when I was just starting out, I met a wonderful man I called Uncle Lee. To me he was *magic.* I don't know how he did it, but he had the ability to go right to a person's core. He simply addressed a deeper level in others than most people do. Uncle Lee was not a professional, but he was a healer. Although then I didn't really know all that word implied, he also was an alcoholic.

One afternoon a bunch of us young seminarians were hanging around whining. What about? About the futility of trying to help people who didn't want to be helped, about caring more for others than they cared for themselves, about how much the system stunk. We talked long and loudly about what we would do to change it. After all, we had been on the street maybe three weeks—

we knew the score. Looking back, I think we were mostly scared stiff. We were in over our heads and had no idea what to do. So, like lots of scared boys, we whistled loudly as we walked through the graveyard.

Uncle Lee heard us and thundered out, "There's not a damn one of you that is any good at all! There's not a sweet man among you. You guys ought to quit before you hurt someone." With that he more or less wobbled away in a huff of offended, whiskey-scented dignity. No matter how drunk Uncle Lee was, somehow he always managed to wrap himself in a cloak of righteous indignation!

After our shock at being scolded, most of us just shrugged off his comments. After all, he was a drunk. What did he know?

He might have had the disease, but he knew plenty. A few years later I came to believe that he was absolutely right. It isn't brains or big ideas that make the difference. Healing does not have to do with degrees and titles. When healing is at issue, it always comes down to a question of sweetness. Sometimes the hammer of change is wrapped in velvet, but the velvet must always be there. Maybe you've heard the old saying, "No one cares how much you know until they know how much you care." That's never more true than in the Dance of Healing. Never more true. Tell me how much sweetness you bring to the Dance, my friend, and I'll tell you how much difference you will make.

As you become more familiar with the Secret, you will know why this is true. When all is said and done, there is only love and love denied. That's it. Sweetness puts you in touch with the heart of the matter. So here's the message from Uncle Lee to you: *strive to be a sweet man (or woman)*.

It was so cold today that my face hurt when I went outside. My cheeks felt like frozen glass that could be shattered into a million pieces by an impact. The grandkids were staying with us, enjoying the frosted-over windows. Was it ever so when you were a child? Today we had a grand time tracing happy faces in the frost. The kids think Grandpa is very clever. I'd press my fingertip to the frost, and of course a small amount of it would melt, sending tiny rivers down the windowpane. Pretty cool! When I showed them I could do it with my nose, they thought I was right up there with the wizards!

We so tend to measure life by the big events. But it is the million and one everyday miracles that create the stuff of our existence. When we get too busy or tired or angry or hurt to hear the music of these miracles, it is time to back off until we can. When we can no longer hear the music, we are no longer healers. Or at least what we are doing at the moment is no longer about healing. It is necessary—no, *essential*—to connect mindfully with the beauty in the world. For me it was those beautiful faces saying in amazement, "Oh, Grandpa, that's cool." If you would be a sweet man, the beauty you find in humanity is your protection. In fact, it's the instrument that awaits your artistry. So find your angels, my friend, and hold them tight. They are your guides.

The secret

Remember Kurt asking me if there was "a secret?" He was looking for some kind of special knowledge or secret wisdom that, like the shaman's spell, made all things possible. Or, if not possible, at least clear.

The answer, my friend, is yes and no. Yes, there is the Secret: *you need new eyes to clearly reveal what it is you are looking at.* But no, there is no secret in the sense that there's a shortcut to healing, a quick fix by magic words that softens hearts and transforms attitudes. I know of no such magic. But I can't tell you how many times—*how many times*—I've fantasized about having a magic stick I could use to touch people who were in terrible pain to effect a healing transformation. Oh, for a "grace stick" that, once touched to heart and mind, would release a resentment, enlighten a pool of darkness, and turn the vision from destruction to creative action!

But that's all fantasy. All any of us can do is throw a stone of goodness in the pool, set the ripples on their journey, and get out of the way. The Secret is to recognize what's right before you. Always, always, if the quest is for healing, what you are looking at reveals the realm of the heart. As I said before, at root, that's all there is when it comes to human well-being—love and love denied. When love is denied, there is a wound, and if that wound is not healed, the bleeding will continue across the pages of every one of our days in an amazing variety of ways. Regardless of the masks of pain and dysfunction, when you look beneath muscle and tissue, you will always find the same process in action. What we are all about—and all that we are about—is hoisting our little sails and praying for a homing wind.

I can't tell you the Truth. You must find your own truth. You must earn your soul on a daily basis by the decisions you make based on the truth you take to heart. All I can tell you is what has proven to be true for me: we, all of us, are hungry for love. Such is the nature of our kind.

Slowly, if you pay attention and keep working at it, this idea will become your basic assumption, the pillar of your philosophy. Healing is always a love story. You will see evidence of it everywhere.

When I was a boy, my father was a plasterer. Those were the days before sheetrock, when plastering walls took great skill. Every house or building we ever went into, my dad would sidle over to a wall, tap it a few times, eye it up to see if it was "straight." For the life of me, I could never see exactly what he was looking for. I never understood what a "straight" wall was. They all looked the same to me. Not to him. He knew what to look for. He'd say, "Not bad," or "The man who did this was an artist." (He considered plastering an art practiced by fellow craftsmen, such as Michelangelo, who worked with wet plaster, too.) Sometimes he'd look and just shake his head. That meant that someone unworthy to call himself a plasterer had worked this wall.

He knew what he was looking at.

A month ago I was with my son-in-law, a professional golfer and a marvelous young man. We were visiting a golf course that was in the process of being created. All I saw was farmland. Not him. As we stood on this little knoll, he looked out and asked, "Can you see it? Right there is the fairway, over here is the tee box, the greens would line up right there, and over there . . . ." Like a total dolt, I could only mumble, "If you say so." All I saw was a place for cows to eat lunch.

He, too, knew what he was looking for.

So must you. It will come to you as naturally as breathing if you allow the vision to sink into your soul. Behind wildly different, unrelated events, your inner eye will come to see the same process unfolding. And recognizing what you are looking at will give you sure knowledge of how to react. What to do—or not to do—will come to you. Certainly, you may not always be right, but you will never be lost.

Even if others don't see what is happening in and around them, you will. Amidst all the noise you will hear a voice. At the heart of all the chaos, you will experience calm and stillness. Behind all the misguided fury, you will be able to touch that tender cord of truth: we all are just trying to get back home. If healing is the issue, then through the distracting noise of misguided efforts, the stumbling around in the dark, you will hear all the various gods speak of God. When the Secret becomes yours, like the carver, no matter how rough the exterior, your artist's eyes will clearly see the flow of the grain at the heart of the wood.

The Secret is recognizing what's right in front of your face. Healers understand that the Dance of Healing is, at its core, always the same. We are born for love, we lose our way, and then we struggle to get back home.

The Dance

Ballplayers call the Big Leagues "the Show." Police officers call what they do "the Job." I hope it is not too glib to call the job of healers "the Dance." In many ways it is much like a dance.

What I mean by this is that people's lives intersect, rub up against each other, pass over, around, and under each other in such incomprehensible, random ways that no human mind could ever orchestrate. That's the Dance.

Yesterday I was asked to speak at our church. Once at the podium, the first thing I did was play a song by Mahalia Jackson. Mahalia has been gone for more than forty years now. When she laid down that song so long ago, she couldn't have known that a church full of strangers would use it to help them find their spiritual path. Our own deeds are the same. How do you know? How could you *ever* know? Each day we send out ripples for ill or good. Once the ripples are in motion, we have no idea what other ripples they will cross, what meaning they will carry, what invitations to a deeper level they will offer.

Last week I conducted one of our regular seminars. Only a handful of people showed up. How disappointed I felt! But see, that attitude is a failure to live up to the Dance. One woman who did show up (I'd never seen her before) got to talking about all the abuse going on in her life. Sad story. I told her that she obviously needed a strong, positive support system. She had no idea, *none,* that there ever was or could be such a thing as a support system. She had no money for professional help and could not imagine a life where people helped people.

Sitting right behind her was another woman, Judy. I knew she was a regular in one of the support groups we founded some fifteen years ago. She said she was there on a fluke, had no intention of coming, but some other plans had fallen through and our seminar just happened to be within a block of her house. The friend who had agreed to meet her at the seminar had failed to appear. So there Judy was—stood up, present for no reason she could think of, actually just kind of passing time. That's the Dance. "Just happened" doesn't exist in the Dance. Why did I feel like hell? Because my plan of working with a decent number of people was not fulfilled. But the Dance isn't about my plan. The Dance is about the fact that there is *the* Plan above, behind, and around my plan. The people there were the ones who needed to be there. Once I got these two women together and talking, I just got out of the way.

Accident? Coincidence? Not if you have a vision of the Dance. It's often said that "coincidence is God's way of staying anonymous." But I've learned to recognize coincidence as God's fingerprints smudging the pages of daily life (like telltale chocolate fingerprints on the refrigerator when the grandkids are visiting). Once you learn to recognize "coincidences," they seem to be everywhere.

Understanding the Dance protects you from all the various ways you can burn out. Take it on yourself to make "the big difference," and you assume a burden that cannot be lifted. The effort, in fact, will break your back as well as your heart. Embracing the Dance is allowing yourself to adopt your proper role—as a note, not the whole symphony. Redirections and expansions of energy are going on behind the scenes that you know nothing about. Planned intersections may be so complex that they are beyond even the most cunning mind. Every once in a while, however, if you look quickly out of the corner of your eye, you may catch a glimpse of the Dance in motion. Like with Mama.

When I was young and just starting out I was working in a black inner city parish in St. Louis. Several sweet, dedicated, young white kids from AmeriCorps Volunteers in Service to America (VISTA) were also working in the neighborhood. One evening there was a neighborhood meeting in the toughest part of this rough part of town. Jill, one of the VISTA kids and as good a human being as you're likely to find in this world, hiked through the ghetto, against advice, to get to the meeting. Just as she arrived, old Mama Woody, all of about 250 pounds of her, came chugging up the street. She was God in black skin if God ever existed. Mama scrubbed floors in an office downtown. Her old hat (honest to God, it had two holes in the brim; why else could they have been cut except for horse's ears?) was perched squarely on her head. She had walked many blocks to get to that meeting and was gasping for air by the time she trudged up to the front of the rundown meeting house. Bits of broken glass, which we called "ghetto diamonds," glistened everywhere. As they crunched under our feet, it felt like stepping on bugs.

In those days big chunks of government money were being funneled into various inner-city projects. But big chunks of money are like big chunks of cheese—they tend to draw out the rats. That's what Mama called the politicians and other exploiters who were after all that money—"them big fat rats." As well as everyone else, she knew that most of that money never made it to "the folk." The rats got it. No way in hell Mama was ever going to see one dime of those grants. That's why she was at this meeting. By raising hell, she hoped to keep the rats from stealing the money from what she called her "babies." "Dem rats can't have my babies' money!" she'd say with passionate intensity. She meant any money that would improve neighborhood kids' chances of getting a decent education or playgrounds or medical care. Mama Woody must have been tired clear to the bone, but there she was, standing on exhausted legs, confronting all the powerful rats, protecting her babies' money. Totally counterculture. In memory, it's a magnificent picture. Breathing fire, she had those rats shaking in their boots. They still got most of the cheese, but Mama made it tough for them.

Some people have high IQs, my friend. Some are smart, slick, sly, or street savvy. And some just know stuff. They *know.* Mama knew. She had a Ph.D. in knowing the heart. You don't get certified or credentialed in this kind of knowledge; no board recognizes it. But it is what qualifies you to be heard. As far as knowing what people are all about at their core, if I had to choose between a college professor who knew all about the theory of personality and the methodology of statistical analysis, or Mama, I'd take Mama every time.

Can you hear this? Can you take Mama's beautiful black face between your hands and stare into her soul? Can you hear her music? Right here is what it is all about: "They can't have my babies' money." Not because she is some wild-eyed crusader addicted to fronting a cause but because of the meaning of the cause. Mama stood tall just because that is who she was. Her presence bespoke a shining spirit, and it was the quality of her spirit that made the difference. *First things first: It's always essence before action.*

When Mama saw Jill walking up, she sternly pulled her aside, rebuking her for being so foolish as to walk those mean streets alone. I watched as she pulled a large butcher knife from her sleeve, telling Jill, "If old Mama gotta carry protection, what do you think you gotta do? You got protection? You ready to use it if you do? If not, you got no business out here."

Mama was a healer. She knew what she was about. She saw the goodness in Jill, the sincere desire. Mama had no wish to extinguish the young woman's flame. After her admonition, Mama replaced her knife, pulled Jill into a warm embrace, and they set off together into the meeting. Can you see it in your mind's eye? *It's the Secret.* It says everything I have to say no matter how many words I offer you. As these two very different women pushed on into the building, I noticed Jill taking hold of Mama's coat. Just one small, frail, white hand reaching out, making contact, grabbing hold of a power much greater than herself. She just needed to hold on to her angel for a while.

Sometimes little things, scarcely noticed or quickly dismissed by most, carry dazzlingly profound meanings. They amaze us, humble us. Just as the mighty oak is contained in the acorn, these people, the most natural and gifted healers, readily sense in the insignificant the fingerprint of all that is. Somehow the bedrock business of life, which is life itself, plays more consistently in their hearts.

How do you put words to that little scene with Mama? All the commitment in the world, all the dedication to struggle, the willingness to go to any length to make a little gain for the Spirit with absolutely no thought of personal gain or fame. Can you see it? Can you feel it? Does the River flow through your soul?

How tired Mama must have been from washing the white man's floors all day! In a place where she would never be welcome. Talk about Mahatma Ghandi! Hers was also a great soul. Hate didn't kidnap Mama. Rage and self-pity didn't murder her soul. With a depth I'm not sure I will ever understand, she just kept plugging along, doing what she could. She tucked her old knife up her sleeve, ready to do whatever it took, and marched up the hill.

It's always about essence. Essence before action. Essence *through* action. Anyone can act. But you can't fake essence. Who we are is where the power is. Who we are makes all the difference. It is the depth of spirit that creates healing, not credentialing, certification, or degrees. All of those things are fine and necessary; they just don't have anything to do one way or another with healing.

Healing isn't about touching minds so much as it is making a connection of the heart. Connecting hearts is about essence. *The banquet is never about what is on the table. It is about who is in the chairs.*

Focus on Jill taking hold of Mama's coat. When you wrap your mind around that simple scene, what does it whisper to you? If you want to know the Secret, there it is. Healing doesn't mean that the pain goes away. Often it doesn't. Sometimes healing doesn't even mean that things are different. Many times they are not—at least not on the outside. What it does mean, more often than not, is that *I am not alone.* And since I am not alone, I find the strength to stand on my own two feet. It means that when I can't get up, I can hold on to you for a moment. When I can't lead, you will let me follow. When all I can do is just sit, someone will be there to sit beside me until I can get up and move on. If you stay in the Dance, you will see this acted out a million times.

Jill had not the slightest idea of what role she should play. She was simply going forward, a lamb in a pack of wolves. The whole story as best I have been able to figure it out in all these years was right there: one small hand hanging on to a tattered old coat wrapped around a pillar of fire, going forward.

There are so many ill winds that blow us away from home! Healing means finding a homing wind. More often than not, those homing winds are aided by, begun by, embodied by, people who just for a time, let us take hold of their coats as they move past us. We hitchhike on their essence.

All this might sound too fanciful or poetic to be real or practical. But poetry speaks to depths that prose will never know. Poetry is the language of the heart, and the heart is where healing happens. Healing is always a love story.

All love stories seem repetitive. That is what held me up for a while as I prepared this section. I had many lesson-stories to share with you, laid them out, then sat back and realized, "Why, hell, they are all the same. It's just one big repetition. How will anybody ever learn anything from that?" So I sat by the door of my cave and waited for the answer to come visit me. It did.

Of course, it is a repetition! There is only one story. In the same story are both the cause and the effect, the bloody knife and heroic effort to stand up yet again. In every story of what we are about—the drama of personal redemption—are the forces that throw us off course. Then comes the homing wind, urging us back to our place at the table. All are valid lessons occurring at different stages of the journey. Lots of stories, but just one process, one journey, one Dance. It drove me nuts until I figured out the difference: the repetition is not in the story but in the focus taken at any given time.

So if you must endure the repetition, it is only because of my too-limited ability to paint the picture. I'm not a very good shaman. The reality of the story being told, no matter how repetitious, is always new, always fresh. It always evokes gasps of gratitude at simply being allowed to take part in the Dance, tears at the overwhelming loss and pain; squeals of joy; stunned, awestruck silence whenever we realize we are in the presence of the sacred—which is anytime we truly witness what is right before us. It's a movie worth seeing again—and you will, because you've already chosen to do so. You wish to be a healer because you have already been captured.

I don't want you to think the Dance is all blood and guts. The Dance is everywhere. Wherever there is life, there is the Dance. Yesterday, for example, we babysat the grandkids. It's always a task to get those two little bundles of energy to take naps. I usually lie down with one, Granny with the other. We read stories and monkey around till they fall off to sleep. I lay there with my soul full of people you will meet later—Old Blue, anorexics begging to go home, Vietnam vets with souls shot full of holes—and right next to me is this little person absolutely bursting with God's purest light, an innocent wearing the flesh of God. It's too much, really— nearly overwhelming. Yesterday I was far more tired than the child beside me. After our stories, I rolled over with my back to him. It's my signal that it's time to slip off. When I do this, he usually likes to put his legs over my side or on my shoulders. He thinks it's funny, I guess, or maybe, to him, it says something like, "I love you." Perhaps for him, it is like putting his feet to a warming fire. I don't know. I don't care. I just love for him to do it. That is the Dance, too.

At any rate, when I was drifting off yesterday I felt some movement. I lifted my head, and there was this little boy trying to pull a cover over me. "Here, Grandpa, you need a cover, too," he said.

Is it too simple? Can you see a connection between this dear act and Mama chugging up the hill?

Two days ago I was on a plane flying out to do a convention for professionals. I jotted down these lines about a half-hour before touchdown. It's a conversation with the Conductor of the Symphony:

"I am tired."

"You try to carry too much."

"The need is everywhere."

"Oh, are you in charge?"

"What should I do?"

"Just show up and don't get in the way."

"I don't understand."

"I know."

"How do I best serve?"

"I told you, show up and move over."

"I'll never get it, I don't think."

"That's okay, little brother, I have a lot of time."

It never ceases to amaze me how often I have to refocus.

※

I wasn't there, but this event was relayed to me by someone who had recently attended an international convention of Alcoholics Anonymous (A.A.). It is one of those "just proud to be part of the Dance" scenes.

There were some fifty people at this gathering who had attained fifty or more years of sobriety. Of this number, three were chosen to address the assemblage of 40,000.

My friend told me that one of the three was a small, thin woman named Ruth. She had what looked like a thousand years of living carved in her face. This tiny, tiny woman stood before the huge throng and began by saying, as everyone does at such meetings, "Hello, my name is Ruth." Swelling back from that vast number, like the tender embrace of warm, gentle arms, came the thundering reply, "Hello, Ruth."

Have you ever lost something important, my friend, something you were frantic to find? Perhaps you were ready to board a flight for your first vacation in ten years, and you couldn't find your plane tickets. Or maybe you lost your car keys when you were desperate to get somewhere. On a far deeper level, maybe you lost your child in a crowded shopping mall with hundreds of people milling around. Can you relate to that state of panic?

Countless people today have lost hope, and along with hope goes any sense of self-esteem. Or is the loss of self-esteem first? So many have lost a belief in today or any enthusiasm about tomorrow. They feel trapped. The missing piece that can't be found torments the heart and hand that seeks it.

Do you recall your supreme joy when you found that which was lost? Even though I wasn't at this specific recovery event, I have been at enough of them to know what was going on. It was the missing piece. In that call and response was the lock and key that today's society is largely missing. Right there was the Secret. If you can see into the depths of the heart, it wasn't just Ruth up there, nor was it just the 40,000 people in the stadium—it was and is *all of us*. It was about what we have lost and how we find it. It was, well, the Secret in harmony.

I've been hurt, lonely, and abandoned. . . .

Hello, Ruth. . . .

I've been lost and didn't know how to find my way home
    . . . *Hello, Ruth.* . . .

I've hurt others so badly and myself worst of all; I've made
    such a mess of my life. . . .

Hello, Ruth. . . .

I've fallen so hard, I don't know if I can get up. . . .

Hello, Ruth. . . .

I've turned everyone against me. . . .

Hello, Ruth. . . .

I know there is no salvation without forgiveness, but how
   can I forgive myself?

Hello, Ruth. . . .

   You name the poison, I'll name the cure: "Hello, Ruth. . . ."

   I know this introductory snippet of an A.A. meeting is often
held up to lighthearted fun in sitcoms these days. I guess anything
is fodder for humor, but I'm very serious in telling you to get your
ear to the ground and listen well. Let Ruth and her band of 40,000
come to visit and stay a while. They speak the truth.

   That truth was born of experience. These people weren't playing at something. They weren't actors. They were coming right
from their heart's experience. Somewhere in that crowd was the
man who for more than three years tried to establish an A.A. meeting in his small town. Week after week he waited all alone at the
announced place and time. No one else ever came. But every week,
he was there on time with his Big Book, ready. Someone asked him
why he would do such an obviously silly thing—keeping showing
up when no one else did. His answer was simple, "When I needed
my first meeting, someone was there for me." So he waited. One
day someone did show up. Then another. Today he carries a lot of
souls around in his pocket. He was at the convention, responding,
"Hello, Ruth. . . ." He knew what he was talking about.

   Ginny was there too. She answers an Intergroup help line in a
Midwestern city. When people are in need of someone to come
help them up because they can't get up themselves, they call
Intergroup, and Ginny answers. She is so old and heavy she can
hardly get around anymore. She told me "the boys" had rigged up
a sheepskin pad by her phone. Why? She needed a place to rest her
arm because leaning on the counter was giving her bruises. Sweet
as a lamb, I'll tell you, but she could raise bloody hell if she called
an A.A. club to find someone to go out on a call and she felt they

were dodging her. Then she'd rage like an avenging angel, "By, God, someone was there for you! You damn well owe it to be there for the next one."

When Ginny shouted back, "Hello, Ruth," her greeting wore the coat of a hundred thousand hours spent on that lifeline she staffed. The richness of her "Hello, Ruth" wasn't about *what* she said, it was about who was saying it.

Alice was there, too. She had lost it all, including her kids, through alcohol, drugs, and prostitution. But, by the grace of God, she had found her way back. Alice knows the difference between here and there. After a meeting one night, I was with her when several other women were complaining about their legs. Too short, they said, too long, too fat, flabby thighs. "Oh, I don't know," Alice calmly said. "Mine reach the ground. That's all I care about." She had finally gotten her priorities straight. I've seen her do magic on some of Ginny's calls that all the Ph.D.s and credentialed folks in the world couldn't do.

When Alice responded, "Hello, Ruth," it came from a depth of the human heart that also produced the old song "Amazing Grace." She was *there.*

Scotty was there, too. He is a tough old double amputee who manages a flophouse that caters mostly to down-and-out recovering people and castoffs in general. Late one night when he was already in bed, he heard a terrible racket outside. It sounded like street punks were trying to roll a resident. If you lived in Scotty's flophouse, you came under Scotty's protection, meaning that no one had better mess with those under his care. Without hesitation, Scotty was out of that bed and charging the punks without bothering to strap on his artificial legs. I can't imagine what that looked like—a guy charging into battle on short stumps—but I can well imagine the protective fire of his eyes; I've seen it often.

When on his mission, Scotty is a man without limits. He'll be there no matter what. Legs or not, he's on his way to take his stand beside you. Through all those tens of thousands of people in the stadium, you can bet there was a bond between Ruth and Scotty. They might not know each other's names or faces, but they know each other's hearts. They both knew they'd make a charge, legs or no, to stand by the other.

Judy was there, too. Judy had sat by her daughter's bedside through her last terrible months. The young woman's life had been wasted by alcohol and drugs, but Judy had never let her daughter go. Never judged her. Never cast her out. With endless motherly love, she stayed right there till the end. "No matter what," Judy told me, "no one should ever have to die alone." With the vision that only healing love generates, Judy said, "Isn't she beautiful?" when she looked at her wasted daughter. Yes, when Judy answered back, "Hello, Ruth," she knew just how much *hello* meant.

People get blown off course. Their deepest needs go unmet. The wounding that most needs healing is always, always festering right there in those unmet needs. Healing is always a love story; it's Judy and Scotty and Ginny and the man who showed up for the meeting because "someone was there for me." Healing is a mother saying, "Isn't she beautiful?" Healing is about finding out where the wound is, because to know where the wound is to know much of the Secret. Most times, the Secret is not revealed on a grand scale of tens of thousands of people at national conventions. Usually, it is so small and quiet that you have to be very still to notice it.

I think of three elderly ladies called Anne, Mildred, and Margaret. Hardly anyone knew they were alive, so few knew when Anne died except for Mildred and Margaret. They had been the three Musketeers of their retirement home. Not in any swashbuckling sense—it was just that the three of them were always seen together by the large window at the end of the hall. Anne suffered a debilitating, wasting disease. Her family could no longer care for her. Mildred was in the beginning stages of Alzheimer's, and Margaret was mentally challenged. None of them fit very neatly into the world of their fellows. All three felt alone—until they found each other. Somehow the connections meshed, and in that unity was the safety and community none of them could create on her own. Hour after hour they sat there, telling stories, relating memories, singing softly, or more often than not, wrapped in silence, yet not alone—not if their companions were on hand.

Then Anne died. For Margaret and Mildred a hole appeared in the universe. They still met by their window, but it was never the same.

This is no big story, no 40,000 voices united in shouting out the Secret. Just three little old ladies getting by by getting together. Yet, if you know how to look, the Secret is as vibrant among them as it was in the packed stadium.

Gary's version of the Secret is just a little story, too, but it thunders with the voice of God. Not too many years ago, Gary won the wheelchair division of the New York City Marathon. A great victory. Greater yet was his earlier victory regarding the quality of his spirit. Not long ago, Gary told me that he always goes to local wheelchair marathons to man the water stations. One of these occasions was a cold day, drizzling rain off and on. Gary was at his post for more than six hours. I can just see him sitting there, rain dripping off the bill of his baseball cap. I asked him why he stayed there so long when it was so miserable out. His comment: "It isn't the people who come by in the first few hours who need encouragement. It is the ones dragging by after four, five, or six hours—however long it takes. Those are the real heroes. They are the ones I want to reach out to."

Do you see what he saw, my friend?

In my mind, I can see him clearly, shivering in his wheelchair, shouting to some sore, tired, out-of-breath athlete, "Be strong! Looking good! Almost there, buddy! You got it now!"

I can just *see* him. Can you recognize the Secret? Do you see how Gary is engaged in the Dance?

Sometimes the clothes the Secret wears are so soaked in blood it's hard to believe. Here is part of a letter I just received from a man in prison. He has not only climbed on the back of the Secret, but he's also been the means of other inmates to do the same. How? By facilitating a program that fosters hope for his fellow prisoners. He says:

> If only you could see the faces of men who have given up all hope. Then, when they get involved in our program, I see a smile return to each frozen face. Hope is generated in a man who has given up! . . . I can say this because I was there. I know the dehumanizing pain each man in here is going through. I have also been beaten, raped, locked in a room for two days without toilet paper. Once I spent four days in a cell with no clothes, and I've seen men killed and gang raped, begging for mercy.

> These guys aren't forced to come to this program. They come because the word is out that this program can change lives forever; it restores their hope. . . .

> I have learned absolute respect for another person's personal boundaries. And I feel the deepest sorrow for any victim of a crime whose boundaries I violated in any way. No one has the right to violate anyone, no matter what. I deserve to be here because of my actions, but I also believe I have the right to the rest of my life. The only amends I can make to some of the people I have

hurt is to turn my life around and never go back to the way it was . . .

We're learning to love, Earnie. You would think prison is the last place in the world a guy could say that, wouldn't you? But it is just what our program teaches. It is the only thing that can turn a life around.

The essence, the Secret, my friend, is in a hundred thousand stories. Each story a face. Each face different, yet the story never changes, as it circles throughout the lives of us human beings. The name of the Secret is love. Can you envision Scotty charging those punks on his stumps? If you think that's something, envision God coming to rescue *you*. There is no darkness He will not enter, no depth He will not plumb, no dysfunction He will not attack. He is with you all the way, no matter what, forever. All you must do is show up. Just show up and say, "Here I am."

chapter 2

AS THE TREE IS BENT . . .

As the tree is bent, so shall it grow.

I hope I'm not beating a dead dog, dear reader, but this point is critical. As obvious as the image of the bent tree is, somehow we seem to continually miss the point.

Who wouldn't agree with the idea that you get out of anything only what you put in to it? We use that concept over and over again in dealing with our kids and employees. We hear it at commencement exercises and in motivational speeches: *There is no free lunch. You will not harvest what you have not sown.*

You want good grades, do your homework. You want a hard body, do your exercises. You want financial security, get rich slowly by consistent saving. You want a good relationship, work at it on a daily basis.

We all know the drill.

A man I'm working with once said, "My dad always told me, 'Keep up with everyone else from Monday through Friday. It's on Saturday and Sunday you get ahead.'" The son followed that advice. Can you guess the healing he is seeking now, some forty years after he bought into that workaholic lifestyle? There's no question he's been financially successful. There's also no question how he got that way—he simply outworked everyone else.

When the goal is personal redemption, balance and realistic expectations are essential. If we would dethrone old king habit and replace him with a kinder model, it is going to take consistent, courageous effort. Whatever the individual's spiritual blockage, it's going to take long, diligent practice to make a bent tree stand straight again. And I'm not talking about achieving perfection. "Perfect" is not an option for us humans. When we have done everything we can—or at least what we are willing to do at this time—all that is left is to strap on our brace, if need be, and limp off down the road. What I am talking about is reaching that bend of the road in the journey when we seriously *want* healing, when we are in a place to do something about it, when we're ready to grow.

Readiness enables us to directly approach the shark bite that was taken out of our soul. To see how that's done, let's take a closer look at some of the presenting problems that people commonly exhibit. Then let's ferret out the underlying wound by passing through symptoms down to the level of cause. You may reject the whole model once you see it, but first, make sure you really *see* it!

It strikes me as insane to think that a wound could be healed before the source of the bleeding is identified; you have to know where the cut is in order to know where to put the Band-Aid. And you also have to find the wound that's really causing the problem; you don't heal a bleeding ulcer by putting a Band-Aid on your cut finger.

Sometimes, to characterize this process, I've used the analogy of picking up downed power lines that are sparking and crackling. Scary, yes, but there's energy in abundance there. I suggest that healing requires grabbing hold of those broken lines even though the sparks are flying. Why? Because all that energy comes from the depth of our yearning for love. It is the most powerful of all motivators!

When love is denied at our most vulnerable time—in childhood—how could we think that disastrous scene wouldn't be crackling with enormous amounts of energy when we revisit it? To approach this domain is frightening indeed. We want to run for cover when we get so close to the dancing lightning. But healing is not a game for the squeamish. If you would put your hand to the beating heart of your life, or someone else's life, you can expect to leave part of your soul there.

As I said before, the Secret is recognizing what you are looking at. What you will discover in this Dance of healing, if you look well, is always the point at which the tree was first bent and tied down. That's where the deformity started—always at the hand of love denied.

Enough theory. Allow me to share four more shadows dancing on the wall of my cave. Actually, these four stepped forward and said, "Let us tell your friends our stories. Let us guide them and show them where to look."

george

Okay, my friend, meet George.

George is the guy standing next to you as you wait for a traffic light to change. He's never been to prison, is not a drug user, pays his taxes, contributes to society. In lots of ways, he is the most ordinary of ordinary people. That's why he stepped up, I guess; his story is the story of Everyman.

What George is trying to heal is a kind of emotional flatline. He's simply unable to feel much. He'd love to be more spontaneous, if only he knew how. After vacationing in Alaska, one of his employees told George about sitting by a postcard-perfect lake, surrounded by quiet beauty, enraptured by a pervasive sense of serenity. It was so great, the man told George, that he'd get up every morning and just shout into the sunrise to express how glad he was to be alive.

George's eyes were terribly sad when he told me, "I've *never* felt like that. I couldn't shout into the sunrise even if my life depended on it. It just isn't in me. Or maybe it's locked away deep inside me in some concrete box of oblivion."

I don't know if there is a more generous man on the face of the earth than George. When the Ronald McDonald House in his city wanted to host a boat ride for families of seriously ill children, they contacted George to pay for it. He was glad to do it. But when it comes to self-compassion, to treating himself with the same loving care he shows others, he hasn't a clue. It isn't that he thinks about it and decides against it. The fact is that he never thinks about it. Self-compassion just wasn't an option.

As the tree is bent, so does it grow.

I could fill several pages with the sad events of George's life. His parents had very little to give. There was no love, no affection, no encouragement, no sense at all of protection or belonging. Life was not safe for George. We'll visit this fundamental question of safety again later when we speak of deep healing. But for now, simply see that *any current, presenting problem is attached with a steely certainty to a bent tree at the person's core.* As obvious and rational as this proposition is, for some reason we seem to have one hell of an aversion to taking it seriously.

Focus on this one scene (in my mind it symbolizes George's walk): George had heard that if you walk barefoot in a rainstorm, you are in danger of being hit by lightning. That's why he would deliberately take off his shoes and socks and walk through wet fields during such storms. He *wanted* to call down lightning.

These are just words, my friend. But stop and think about them. See them on the outside and the inside. How hurt, how sad, how lonely does a little boy have to be to call down lightning upon himself? *Of course,* the man he is today feels dead when it comes to accepting his right to joy and celebration. How else could that little boy have survived except by killing his feelings? His emotional starvation didn't seem to affect his feelings for others. George, in fact, has acute feelings of generosity and empathy for others. He would fly into the mouth of hell to help someone he saw in need. What died in George was the ability to have such emotions for *himself.* Self-compassion became impossible when he was just a little boy, hoping that lightning would end his sadness.

Remember the old image from Sunday school? When we die, we stand before God who holds the book listing all our good and evil deeds. George is no saint, but if that image is true, the list of what he has done for others would be a long one indeed. Yet ask George if he thinks he may be admitted to eternal peace when he dies. Sadly, he'll say he doesn't think so. Of course, that isn't just what he *thinks,* it is what he *feels.* And those feelings are the petrified emotions of fifty-plus years of praying for a good lightning storm to come around. The tree was bent and so it grew.

Later, when we talk about the Hoop, we'll study the dynamics of core wounding. For now the only point I want to make is this: present pain is not an accident, not if it is repetitive. Anything can happen *once.* But if the negative events, behaviors, or feelings are an abiding issue, a recurring pattern, you can bet the farm there is a bent tree deep down inside. You can also be sure there was a toxic, loveless wind that forced that tender tree to the ground and tied it there.

vickie

Vickie looks like a still-cute middle-aged cheerleader. Everyone loves her because she's fun, bubbly, and wise in many ways. She is the kind of woman who, if you have a daughter heading into dangerous waters, you hope your daughter will talk to. Vickie gets through to people. There is a good dose of street smarts in her. Again, as with George, the particulars can wait until later. My point here is that Vickie is eminently normal. She works with the PTA, is a homeroom mother at school, does some work with the Big Sister program.

Last week I "just happened" to be at the office in the evening. (I am almost never over there after dinner.) The phone rang. At night, I usually let the machine pick up calls. After all, I'm there to get something done. I don't want phone calls messing up my work schedule.

Are you smiling?

Remember the Dance? There are my plans, and then there is the Plan. I'm telling you, my friend, that's how it is!

Well, I answered the phone before I could catch myself. Apparently, that was Schemer's doing. Schemer is that mysterious mover behind the scenes, the one who secretly orchestrates the Plan and involves you in it. Have you guessed it? I'm talking about God here. The caller was Vickie. She is a loving single mom, but her choice of men stinks. She wanted to tell me that she had been beaten up again.

Vickie had been going out with a huge guy—six-four, about 250 pounds. (She maybe weighs 110.) They were going to be married and were even having a house built. He was a nondrinker, but apparently, he didn't need liquor to lose control. He figured Vickie was his possession, so when she failed to measure up to his criteria of acceptable behavior, physical punishment was justified. In that telephone call, Vickie admitted that he had an "anger issue."

It's all too much, this whole human drama of sweet, lovable, so-good people pounding the hell out of each other, creating vicious cycles that spin down through the years, generation after generation.

The point here is not what Vickie and I talked about; it is how her situation came to be. It is about her journey in life and the fact that for all the variations in all of our journeys, *there is only one story*. As Vickie's tree was bent, so it grew.

George and Vickie could have been siblings. There were some differences, but the basic story line was the same. In Vickie's case, there was a lot of physical abuse. Apparently her parents, especially her mother, had no great qualms about smacking Vickie around. Long before the night she called me, Vickie knew all about getting thrown into walls. She told me that her first marriage, which had lasted nine years, was filled with physical abuse. Once she called her mother after a beating. The advice her mother gave her? Stop being a crybaby and making trouble.

Here's another snapshot to focus on—it tells the whole tale: Vickie recalled in childhood how excited she'd been about her first Holy Communion. Her family was extremely religious. (Poor old God! Just imagine the foul behavior undertaken in his name!) Anyway, Vickie told me she was all decked out in her new white dress, white patent leather shoes, her little anklets, the kind with lace at the top. But before the family left for church, she did something that set her mother off—and got smacked in the face. The blow split her lip, which bled all over her communion dress.

That's it. Picture the bloody first-communion dress. Focus on the symbolism of first Holy Communion—all the love, purity, and peace it is meant to represent, all the comforting safety of holy ritual and a loving God. Think how heightened all of this must have been for a little girl who had never experienced safety. If your own parent makes you bleed, who can you trust to protect you? How could you then ever know anything of self-compassion or learn the means of creating personal safety? Just get a fix on this sweet, beautiful, light-filled child standing before the mirror looking at the blood all over her first-communion dress. No doubt she got blamed for ruining her dress, embarrassing her parents, and "ruining the day."

As the tree bends, we learn to lay low, to cover up. We learn to get along by hiding our broken parts from most people. We laugh, we sing, we live our life, but unless the bent tree is set right, part of our insides remain crooked. This deformity will make its presence felt sooner or later. It can't be otherwise.

What happens when life takes us to an area that requires the use of skills that were never learned? Skills like the ability to choose someone safe for a relationship, the emotional freedom to sing to the sunrise, or just go from day to day with an abiding sense of well-being. The fact is, we *can't*. It is simply not possible. Where the foundation should be, there exists only a jagged, perhaps bloody, hole.

Just last night I used Vickie's story in a seminar—changing her name, of course. The image of the little girl bleeding on her communion dress was potent. Some eyes in the crowd were wet, some crackled in fiery indignation, some were swimming in saddened empathy. Vickie isn't the only one who has ever bled on her new dress.

I made the point as best I could, as I am doing now. Whatever you think of Vickie's story, in a sense it is *everyone's* story. All of us may not have suffered such physical abuse or its later consequences of buying into carbon-copy abusive relationships, but the process is the same no matter what caused the wounds.

I told the crowd (the seminar was on self-esteem) that the only reason any of us comes to self-esteem seminars or uses any self-improvement books or tapes is *because we are not where we want to be*. Why? Because we are somewhere else, a place in need of healing. How did we get there? We got fixated at some point of hurt. Whether that hurt is represented by a startling image such as blood on a communion dress, or a less spectacular, chronic, grinding experience of another version of love denied, it is all the same.

By no means is it always unloving parents who do the damage. Callous abuse and indifference is rife on playgrounds, in schoolrooms, and in society as a whole. Bullies and brutes abound. Sadly, many toxic sibling relationships cause lifelong injury. Which is to say nothing of the screaming needs that went unmet simply because they weren't recognized. Or perhaps someone *did* have a clue about your plight, but didn't have the mental or emotional wherewithal to take action. It doesn't matter whether your wounding was dramatic or much more subtle. The process doesn't change. The story is the same for everyone. George has his story, so does Vickie. It is always easy to see cause and effect in someone else's story. What is *your* story? Where and how was your tree bent? And how is that bent tree making its presence known today?

Real Heroes

I've got to tell you this! I try to take life as it comes, but I saw a book in the bookstore a few hours ago that still makes my blood boil. Right there, at eye-level, was a new self-help book by a big-name author. Lots of publicity. Beneath the title on the cover was the sizzler: "A quick, easy system of personal change." The guy should be doing hard time!

It's *so* dishonest to tell people that the process of personal redemption is quick and easy. You don't get out what you don't put in. To foist such unrealistic expectations on people is to set them up for certain failure, which creates shame that intensifies the damage done by the bent-tree event in the first place. *Never* listen to glib messages like that, my friend, especially when you're at your most vulnerable.

It's one thing to extol the value of doing healing work. It is fine and true to trumpet to high heaven the joy waiting behind the breakthrough. But to tell people that the journey is quick and easy is a fraud of the worst sort. Tell Mama Woody how quick and easy her path is. Tell Scotty charging forward on his stumps, or tell George or Vickie how easy it is to reverse the damage of the bent tree. Nonsense! They are real heroes. Talking quick-fix healing is mockery of the real thing—an insult to those who patiently trudge the good path.

Excuse me, my friend. I need to step back, take a couple of deep breaths, and find my center.

I hear a whisper seeping up through all this racket in my mind. It's the Master of the Dance telling me to quiet down. I hear! I hear! I hear!

But "quick and easy," my ass.

Lester

Lester is a guy I met in prison. A friend of mine and I flew up there a few weeks ago. This prison was using a lot of our material. An inmate who often writes me said what an honor it would be "for the guys to meet you." It's all in the Dance, my friend. It's all about Schemer pulling out a costume for us to wear. If, for whatever reason, something I've done has made it an honor for guys to meet me, then who am I to deny or reject that offer? It isn't about me. It's about Schemer pulling strings behind the scenes to fill the hoisted sail taking us home. Accepting the invitation was a no-brainer. So off we went.

The friend I am talking about flies a small Comanche Piper Cub. He's been in A.A. for more than thirty years and would fly that damn plane into the devil's mouth to carry the message, any-where, any time. His eyes got so big when I mentioned that some inmates had asked us to visit. "I'll get the Comanche fired up," he immediately responded. "You tell me when you want to take off." *I'll get the Comanche fired up* . . . like it was a magic flying carpet or something. In a way, I guess it is. In the sense that all healing is magic because it comes from a connection of the heart, and every-thing that comes from the heart has an element of magic to it.

I know I'm being wordy here, but you should have seen that flight. Just thinking about it makes me laugh. I don't like to fly, especially not in small planes. The view is great, but if you hit rough weather, the plane pitches around and makes you feel like you're trapped in a pinball machine. But what the heck? I figured that if I was trying to be faithful to the Dance, I may as well be willing to strap myself into that torture machine.

I was hanging onto the straps on both sides of the cabin, trying not to get sick. My friend seemed to be unaware of the bouncing. He is a big man who really doesn't quite fit into the pilot's seat. His head was right up against the cabin roof, and his knees were almost up to the steering wheel (or whatever it's called on a plane). Yet I can hardly explain how excited he was! Whenever I dared to hold my head up and open my eyes, I got a good view of him from the rear and side. He was just humming along, eyes shiny, practicing what he was going to tell his brothers. "They're my brothers," he said, "because a thousand times, a *thousand* times, I could have wound up right there with them for drunk driving, killing someone, or other mishaps." He didn't care to share more about those mishaps, and I didn't want to hear. The man is a glorious sidekick. I could wish you nothing more than a companion like him when you go out charging windmills.

Anyway, once we arrived we met with about a hundred of the one thousand men at this facility. After our sharing (which was all about hope, the need for taking responsibility for our lives, and the strength of a spirit that decides to strive for freedom), there was time for questions and answers and just general shooting the breeze. That was when I met Lester.

Lester told us he was forty-three, that he had been in and out of jail since he was fifteen or so and constantly in trouble before that. He said that this time around he's learned a lot in prison. In fact, he's made a commitment to straighten his life out and help others. He joined A.A. inside and goes to every kind of self-help program offered.

Lester looks like the guy who coaches your local Little League baseball team. Balding and thin, he has a soft voice and a rather intense manner. He's not a monster—I saw no horns or tail. But I did see the effect of the bent tree growing sideways, parallel to the ground instead of poking a hole in the sky as it was meant to do. Yes, Lester has done terrible things. He doesn't deny it. Perhaps he's done his own version of knocking a Vickie into a wall. But for all I could tell, he is struggling as mightily as he can to turn it around. Turn what around? You tell me. Whatever his crime, whatever he has done while lost on his path, can you tell me, for certain sure, where it all started? Yes, the deformity always takes root in love denied.

As I gave you a single image from George's and Vickie's walks, here is one from Lester's. He said that as a child, his hurt and pain was so bad that he would often go out into a field, dig a hole, crawl in, pull leaves over on top of him, and hope no one would ever find him. He was practicing being invisible, as had George and Vickie.

Stop. Freeze that frame as if you're running a home movie. Look at the scene. Lester didn't *always* have a prison number. Watch this slight, lovely little boy walk out into the woods. (Or did he run or slink? Perhaps *flee* is a better word.) Watch the movie. He digs a hole. You wonder as you watch, "Well, maybe he is playing the kiddie's fantasy of digging a hole to China. We did that a time or two." But no, he digs the hole and crawls in. His two bony little arms reach out and scoop leaves over the all too real-looking grave he's dug for himself.

Let yourself sink inside that little boy's soul. Pass through his tired but determined eyes to the state of his spirit. Look at the shadows on his wall. What do you see? What do you feel? It won't be long before that brutalized child reaches out in kind to brutalize others. Then we'll shout, "Shoot the bastard!" And who will we have shot? The little boy hiding in his self-made grave because life was too painful?

Like all of us, Lester has free will; he made his own decisions and must be held accountable for his behaviors. He knows that. That's not the objective of this exercise. Our goal is to understand the process of how that happens. Until we understand, we won't be able to help in this most important and precious of all human events, in the personal redemption of healing.

You can't visit a prison and not be overstimulated. There is just too much going on, too much to take in. I guess that is why so many inmates just shut down. If you don't grow calluses, you disintegrate. Of all the things that were said or unsaid, of all the looks in the eyes, the body postures, and hand gestures (talk about shadows on the wall!), what kept coming back to me time and time again on the long flight back was the image of little Lester digging that hole. I bet there isn't a guy there—or any other man or woman or child in any kind of controlled environment—who didn't, in one way or another, crawl right in there with him, seeking safety, hoping to become invisible.

Helen

If George is the man standing next to you at the traffic light waiting to cross the street, Helen is standing on the other side. She is single, almost fifty, never married, a college graduate, but just getting by doing clerical and secretarial work. Helen is slight with well-cut hair kept blond "with help," as she says. She is bright, cheerful, always smiling, a favorite of her family and friends. Not a little eccentric, she is the life of every party.

Helen's issue, or problem, is the *abiding sense of failure*. This sense, or feeling, is her primary reality, the context in which she lives. Every once in a while the veil might lift a bit, but never for very long.

Helen more or less constantly feels that she missed the mark and is a disappointment. She habitually finds it very difficult to make decisions, routinely defers to others' opinions or wants, and lives in daily fear that others will take her to task for the failures she never quite understands. For all her lighthearted banter, Helen is afraid nearly all the time. Afraid she will say or do the wrong or "dumb" thing, afraid others will see behind her defenses, and, mostly, afraid that they'll discover that she just doesn't "get" what everybody else seems to understand effortlessly. So she pretends. Like illiterates who become adept at pretending to read, Helen has a whole repertoire of techniques to fake normalcy and okayness. She is a consummate actress and always in pain. Can you see the bent tree?

Helen sold her soul to get acceptance from a father who had none to give. There was never any overt abuse. She wasn't hit or physically brutalized in any way. But she was neglected, ignored, or constantly corrected. Never a pretty child, at least in her own opinion, Helen didn't have either nice clothes or the warm affection of parents to communicate a sense of beauty far beyond the reach of nice clothes. Maybe she was oversensitive or simply more needy than other children. Who is to say? And what difference does it make? The bottom line is that she didn't get what she needed; the tree was bent. The fruit of that tree was this abiding sense of worry, fear, inadequacy, and shame.

Helen sometimes fears she's crazy. She is not. She's no more "one of them," or "sick," than any of the rest of us. She is a functional, contributing member of society. But she is also grievously wounded and in search of healing from a wound she can't understand or even identify.

It's the Secret, my friend, the Dance: as the tree is bent, so it grows. What is sown will emerge. Recognize what you are looking at. At first someone else teaches us, then *we* teach it to ourselves, tying our own tree to the ground all on our own. How? By continuing to create situations where the same toxic, soul-deadening lessons are drummed into us time and time again. *We* take that tender baby flesh, wrap barbed wire around it, and pitch it into our subconscious times without number. Then we wonder why "this thing always happens to me," as though it is an accident.

Well, if we don't understand the process, I guess it does seem like an accident. But it isn't. It *was* caused, then it *is* caused. So much of healing, at least the cognitive part, requires us to understand *why* the consequences of our lives are forgone conclusions. It means becoming aware of the machinery creating them. Think about it. A Christmas-tree cookie cutter will never stamp out anything but Christmas-tree-shaped cookies.

I know very well that the Dance is about God's Plan, not just *my* plan. But I still feel so, I don't know, kind of frustrated, defeated, inadequate, too small for the task at hand. I just reread these four vignettes. I know these people. They are *so much more* than my paltry little descriptions of them. That's the trouble with poetry. No one writes a poem; the poem uses the poet to tell its own story. The vision is always greater than the words used to describe it. So the poet is left with the ache of knowing he was such a poor servant of the vision.

Well, tough rocks. What's so is so. The only way I know to make progress is to pick up your bucket and keep going up the hill.

As I reread this section, a picture formed in my mind, an image of what it means to have the tree *not* bent. It's just a snapshot, really, but in its soul it's the whole story.

A few winters ago, our whole family took a week's vacation at a fancy resort with a big, lovely indoor swimming pool. The grandkids and I spent a lot of time there. Montgomery, then three, decked out in his Barney the Dinosaur life jacket, had some doubts about jumping in. "Come on," I said, standing chest deep in the water. "Jump! Grandpa will catch you. I won't let you sink."

After a bit of coaxing, he managed a small, safe jump close to the side. And, of course, his experience was that he *was* caught. He did *not* sink. "Hey," he figured, "this isn't bad."

It wasn't long before he was imitating Evel Knievel, daring one death-defying jump after another. He'd get back as far as he could from the pool's edge, run at a mad pace, and leap like one of those flying squirrels you see on the Discovery Channel. He'd literally launch himself. Never once did Grandpa let him sink to the bottom. Montgomery learned to trust.

George never had that opportunity. He needed to be caught a million times over, but he was dropped so often and fell so hard that he called down lightning on his own head. He learned fear, as did Vickie with her bloodied communion dress and Lester in his leafy homemade grave and poor little Helen who wanted nothing more than to be her dad's pretty princess. Every human being on earth who seeks healing faces fear in one form or another. I picture my grandson's sparkling little body flying through the air like a young salmon flashing in the sunlight. Somehow, just as the oak is in the acorn, the whole story is revealed in that picture. The whole of our spiritual potential is there, with the breath of God trying to fill our sails. Behind the masks of our differing circumstances, we are all Odysseus plowing through the wine-dark sea, seeking home.

Once you see and accept the pattern, there will be consequences. One of the razors that can shred your soul is to witness the mistreatment of children and to watch the tree being bent right before your eyes. Because now you *know* that this is not just the tragedy of the moment, but seeds being planted that will bear future fields of tears. And it is so prevalent!

About twenty minutes ago I heard a district attorney being interviewed on the radio. I pulled over and wrote down his words. "When thirteen- and fourteen-year-olds shoot people," he said, "we always find that they were witnesses or victims of violence for many years before they pulled the trigger. These kids lost or never had the sense that the finger that pulled the trigger shoots real bullets that have irreversible consequences."

As the tree is bent. . . .

The future is now. The adults of tomorrow are the trees being bent today. Untold millions don't have the slightest idea of home or community, of self-compassion or the security of having a net under them. Many have no fear—for the appalling reason that they have no concept of personal safety, either gained or lost. If your own safety counts for nothing, what is there to fear?

My heart just breaks when I see, listen to, or think about the endless stream of children whose hearts are being torn to shreds by love denied. I hope we will meet someday along the road to healing. But it will no doubt be when they have hurt themselves, and others, so badly that they are forced to their knees.

I'm ending this now because it makes me too sad to think about it when there's so much work yet to be done. Talk about ghosts in the shadows! Sometimes it's just too much to take in.

I just spent some time with a colleague whose approach to the soul is through poetry and art therapy. He's had great success with prison populations using this method. According to him, poetry and art tap into the source of emotions that have become frozen through trauma. That's sure true.

Bear (that's his nickname) is as big as a house. He showed me some of "his guys'" work. Beautiful, beautiful expressions. Certainly not always joyful, but beautiful. Real.

There are *many* avenues to the soul, many methods of liberation. Some people get so enamored of a certain way they forget that *all* the kinds of methodologies are but various feathers on the wings of the same bird.

Case in point: after church last week a totally committed therapist was telling me (with great fervor) that the only way to help seriously hurt people was with psychomotor, or body work. I know other people who swear by hypnosis. Another man well into recovery from cancer claims that nothing makes much difference until you change your diet. Many find New Age philosophy and techniques their royal highway, while others, mainly men, seem to have found something important they had lost by losing themselves in the rhythm of beating a drum and passing of a talking stick. An American Indian friend of mine still talks of singing "the Blessing Way" and "the Healing Way." "The drum," he says, "is the heartbeat of the Earth. By dancing, we are grounding ourselves in Mother Earth." He is a soaring spirit, so obviously his way works for him.

Another hero of mine, Brother Mac, a Jesuit, for many years ran a treatment modality within a recovery center at a state mental hospital. His special program was for those who just could not stay sober. Some of these patients had spent more years in treatment than many of you have been alive. I asked Mac how he could possibly stay in good spirits when he knew his efforts would most likely fail. He just looked at me, gave me his crooked smile and said, "I don't fail. Every day these guys stay sober is a victory. Besides, who is to say what goes on in their souls? My job isn't to judge success or failure. It is just to be there and open a door."

Mac's path relies on humor. He believes in laughter. In a truly marvelous manner, his spirit always seems to be laughing. In the middle of one story he got laughing so hard he almost fell out of his chair. Before he got sober, he once finished a night of drinking, novices in tow, standing on the stage of a strip joint, singing along with the dancers. As punishment, he sputtered happily, his superiors sent him to sober up in France's wine country. "Until I finally got off the stuff, I didn't draw a sober breath for five years," he said. Somehow Mac finds life, including its temporary failures, hugely entertaining.

Look at it this way. *Any* way that works is the right way—for now. Who knows where your path will lead tomorrow? But look closely and tell me if all these various singers aren't ultimately singing the same song. Don't all of them seem to be different harnesses for the same horse? We are all created to survive in love. We get lost. We get stuck. We get called. We get up. We get going. Aren't all of these modalities just God's finger beckoning us down a road we can see only darkly? Behind all of them, can't you just see God "firing up the Comanche" that we might take off into infinity? It seems so clear to me!

As the tree is bent, so it grows. As it grows, a hoop is formed. And encompassing our individual hoops is a larger one—the Hoop that rests in the hand of God.

I thought this chapter was done. Then this popped out: It's 5 A.M., and I'm on a plane to Texas. After getting up at 3 A.M. to make the flight, I fell into a familiar zone. Maybe it's caused by sleep deprivation or just the stress of travel. But whatever the combination of factors, when I'm sitting on these cramped, dark planes I perceive an almost surrealistic atmosphere. Everything around me seems rather disjointed and dreamlike. Some 35,000 feet below are tiny pinpricks of light. To me they look like lightning bugs, but I suppose they are little cities or manufacturing plants.

People all around me are snoring softly. I wonder where they're all going. What are their stories? Who are they going to meet, and what are their circumstances? I sit here in the dark, thinking, wondering, waiting for some visitor to come through my open door.

Two pictures keep merging and then separating in my mind. Somehow, they get all mixed up, taking on aspects of each other. I want to tell you about them.

cricket

Cricket is a very beautiful mother-to-be (soon!). She's been a friend of my stepdaughter's since her earliest college days. I always loved Cricket. She is and was just as sweet, honest, and down-home good as they come. Who knows why we are so strongly attracted to some people? Perhaps we have inner magnets we know nothing of. Maybe I was drawn to her because I never had biological children of my own. Maybe, I don't know. But Cricket is very special to me.

Any day now she is going to have twins. She's already named them Nick and Sam. Cricket looks as big as a house and she's very uncomfortable. But the most compelling thing is the profound sense of life swirling out of and around her. Being with her makes me feel like I am standing on holy ground, perhaps somewhat like Moses said he felt on Sinai. New life! All that potential, all the enfleshed spirit, truly the miracle that birth, life, and starting over is all about.

Feeling like the Beast before the Beauty, I have, stumbled-tongued, asked Cricket now and again how she feels about all "this." I asked her once if she ever feels overwhelmed at the reality of carrying new life in her. At the time she was having a bad day. Whatever wonder there might have been in her spirit had been pulled under by a sore back and aching legs. So I don't know what she thought or felt at that time. I just know the sense of wonder and beauty that surrounds me whenever I am around her. Of course, she doesn't know any of this, but I suppose she will if she ever reads these pages. It's strange how rarely our really important thoughts ever get said out loud.

Anyway, I think of those babies, knowing the family they will be born into, and I can sense all the warm fuzzy clothes, decorated rooms, mountains of toys. I look up through the babies' eyes and see only adoring, wonder-struck faces looking back at me.

The awesome connection of vibrant life and welcoming community is palpable in my heart and soul right now. If Cricket doesn't deliver today, they will induce labor tomorrow. The babies are coming! In a strange but real way, I feel a tiny sliver of belonging there. Cricket doesn't really know me much better than the guy at the gas station. Yet somehow I feel a part of her delivery. In an indefinable way, I am traveling down that road with her. I might be physically distant, but I am right there with her.

mickey mantle

The second image that runs through and overlays this scene is a taped interview I once saw with Mickey Mantle. It was done before he was deathly ill, but after he got out of alcohol rehab. (As one of his eulogists said, "He had some rough innings but a hell of a ninth.")

The interviewer was a young woman. She was long on looks but short on experience. Mickey was his sincere, unpretentious self, honest and humble. There was nothing to hint at a public versus personal persona. In fact, I got to laughing, just thinking of what he, Billy, Whitey, and Yogi would do with a word like *persona*.

Anyway, Mickey talked about visiting one of his married sons shortly after leaving treatment. The son and his wife had just had a baby. Mickey told the young woman interviewing him that he couldn't hold the baby. There was just something about the innocence, vulnerability, and purity of the tiny child that he couldn't allow himself to get close to.

The young woman scoffed. She thought it was a con. How could the great Mick, a world-famous celebrity, the baby's own grandfather, not bring himself to hold his own progeny? He could power a ball five hundred feet to the roof of Yankee Stadium; surely he was not serious about being unable to hold a baby. As I said, the interviewer was very young.

Those who have been in the dark a long time understand how frightening the light can be. There is a huge, sometimes alarming, difference between hard and soft, dark and light, ugliness and beauty. It's easy to get stuck on the wrong side of the fence. Once that happens, you feel very uncomfortable with the opposite. A person can greatly appreciate the beautiful and still be trapped by the ugly limitations of the bent tree. A toxic wind blows through consciousness, saying, "You don't deserve to even get close to something so beautiful" or "It is for others." Frankly, you're downright afraid that somehow you'll damage or dirty something that was too good for you in the first place.

So what's the conclusion, this merging of Cricket and Mickey? I don't know. Maybe there isn't a conclusion. But both came to me in this speeding aluminum tube rushing through the dark. They came through the same open door and stood there side by side—totally different, yet somehow connected.

chapter 3

THE HOOP

I JUST GOT BACK FROM MY MORNING WALK AROUND THE POND. Lovely. At this time of year the pond sends off a haze of mist in the early morning light. The effect is kind of eerie or mystical. Otherworldly. But then I guess that depends on the world we live in. Anything different from what we are accustomed to is "otherworldly."

My problem with walking is that my mind gets going so fast, I can't keep up with the chatter. About ten steps into the jaunt, I start thinking of things I want to tell you, people you should meet, experiences I want to share so we can talk about them later. Some folks love to share fine wine as they philosophize about the good life. Good on them. Healers' "fine wines," though, tend to be victories of the spirit. All those glorious moments when death gets poked in the mouth are the hospitable offerings of those who would be custodians of the soul.

But it's time to get started, isn't it? After the Secret, the Dance, and tied-down trees comes the Hoop.

Let me lead you to the Hoop.

Not long ago, a client who is Jewish told me that his rabbi said, "All that's needed for a happy life is the Torah and a trade."

Torah and a trade. Pretty good, huh? Using different words, Freud said pretty much the same thing. He said that *love and work* are what people needed most. Centuries before that, a great religious order—the Dominicans, I believe—adopted *ora et labore,* "prayer and work," as their motto. At a recent seminar I attended, the presenter named these as the three most basic needs: safety, caring, and a chance for success. Essentially the same message over the centuries.

I have used this line for decades: "When talking of human well-being all there is is love and love denied." It seems to me that all the emphasis on work in the world, without the balance of genuine love, leaves us deformed as hell. Without love, a person can become a magnificent work machine but have no kind of a life. On the other hand, a person whose solid foundation has been built by love automatically works to contribute to the fabric of society.

All well and good, but here is the healer's question, regardless of the words used: what happens to the spirit of the person who is denied basic needs? It's one thing to say "Torah and trade" or "prayer and work"—yup, that's what we need. But what if the person's most basic need has been denied? What happens then? What wound is created when the tree is tied down? What faces might it wear? Are such wounds healable? And if so, how?

This is what brings us to the Hoop, my friend. Our topic is healing. The need for healing is created from the wound of love denied. Let's not quibble over words when life's red blood is pumping out of a tear in the soul!

Again, the Secret, knowing what you are looking at. Study the Hoop I'm about to describe. See if it makes sense to you. Test it out on your own experience, the ultimate yardstick.

Notice, my friend, that the Hoop is not a solid thing as if it were made of metal. Instead it is an entity of the spirit, continually being braided of many strands. Once you begin to recognize this process, this Hoop, you will find that you can jump in at any point and still not be lost. Any slice of life, any experience you encounter or come to recognize in yourself, will fit along one of the strands of this Hoop. Sit with it reverently, and it will tell you its secret.

I am inviting you to journey to a deeper level of the Secret. Peer beneath the apparent face of the surface event and see what is in motion. In the same event you can see those lost and those hurt, those stuck and those hearing the call to rise up and get going. Sometimes you will focus on the healer's presence in the story. At other times, perhaps deeply hidden, yet as obvious as the sun at noon if you learn to look, is the sweating, smiling face of a hard-working God.

I've spent a lot of time mulling over how to be clear about this. Many a walk was taken up with answering your anticipated exasperation: "Hell, all these stories are the same! How am I ever going to learn anything if all the stories are the same?"

Of course they are the same! There is only one story to tell. Only the strands in the Hoop are different. And difference is not in the story but in where you choose to focus as the story is unfolding.

No matter how well or poorly I do my job, you will return time and time again to the magic of these stories. If you would be a healer, that is who you are.

Let us visit the Hoop. It looks like this:

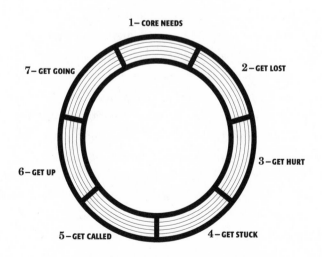

core Needs

Do you remember this old comedy routine? A seriously ill man is lying in a hospital bed surrounded by worried visitors. An air hose runs into his oxygen mask. Then suddenly the man begins thrashing about. His visitors look around in panic. What does the patient need? They all want to help, but no one knows what to do. Finally they figure out from the man's frantic gestures that he's asking for a note pad. He writes, "Someone is standing on my air hose!"

The point is clear. No matter what else is wrong with the guy, if his fundamental need for air is denied, all other problems become trivial. Any other complaint is forgotten at that moment. He's done for if he doesn't get oxygen.

Here's another example. Slam your finger in a car door and whatever else you were thinking about disappears immediately. Whether you're at a funeral or a wedding, winning the lottery, or losing your job, the pain in your finger commands your attention.

So it is with human spirits. *The most basic human need always takes priority.* Whatever else is going on, that bedrock need pulses in the human heart. All is well if the need is met. But let something strangle this vital pulsation and the whole world shrinks to the size of this fist-sized muscle.

The same goes for healing. *So many things* can be going on— so many "presenting issues," so many approaches, so many confusing theories, so many variable conditions, so many different agendas. I caution you not to be distracted, my friend. *Go to the core.* Never lose sight of that vital, pulsing priority. If you can keep your heart's finger on this pulse, you will never be lost or wander too far from the healing way. Knowing this is knowing the Secret.

So what is this pulse, this beating? It's the hunger for love, my friend. That is what our most basic need is—for love and belonging.

How do I say this? Behind all your schooling, all the theories of personality development and statistical analysis, under and behind all the office politics, all the faults and flaws we bring to the Dance, healing is *always* about finding, or rediscovering, that central core, that island buried deep within all of us that is *most* of who we are. Why? Because if access to that island is blocked, as the man's air hose was, everything else goes awry in a variety of ways.

I realize how simplistic and Pollyanna this may sound. But from the bottom of my heart, I can tell you that it is true. I've looked into the eyes of many, many dangerous people—the kind who scare society silly and cost us all billions of dollars. In essence, all of them say there is only one thing that *ever* made a difference: finding their way back to this core. I've heard rock-hard teenage and pre-teenage gang members say exactly the same thing. The gang gives them a sense of family, of belonging. We can study gang behavior until we are broke and exhausted and filled with despair, but until that heavy foot "gets off the air hose," it is all a study in futility.

I've watched people with terminal AIDS step out from the shadows on the golden bridge of supportive relationship. Their sickness couldn't be cured, but their loneliness could. Healing began when someone was there to walk with them. I've seen families torn to shreds for one reason or another, and I've seen miracles of reconciliation. Those miracles are always about a breakthrough, a finding of one's way back to the core from which and of which we are made. Many, many times I've sat with hard-headed realists who called all this love stuff "soft" or "stupid," without realizing that I was sitting with them because their lack of this supposedly "soft" stuff was destroying them.

Although the shadows are jumping with people who want your heart, one man in particular comes to mind right now. This man was a powerful lawyer. If clout had a face, it was his. There wasn't much he couldn't make happen if he wanted. But there we sat—me, his seventeen-year-old daughter, and his mighty self, powerless as a blind kitten. Unknowingly, the man had cannibalized the daughter's self-esteem to feed his need for power. Whenever he was around, he ran his home like an army barracks. As a young child, the girl had no voice. But that was no longer true. Now she was hitting back. She'd finally figured out how to punish this powerful/powerless man for denying her what her core had most needed all those years. She wasn't old enough to understand that he hadn't given her love because he had so little to give. To her, the screaming priority was her own emptiness. But now, at this counseling session, her emptiness was filled with rage, and she was crucifying him. I'm pretty sure that no one in the world could talk to that man the way she did and get away with it. But what could he do? In his own paralyzed way, he really did love his daughter. And he was smart enough to see that because too much damage had been done, she was slipping way into the shadows. It's "early days" in therapy for both of them; I don't know if she'll ever come back. Some don't. When they do, it's always because enough healing has taken place to create the bridge that only love can build.

In terms of well-being, all there is is love and love denied. Why? Because if healing is the issue, that's all there is.

GET LOST

If the need to love and be loved is not adequately met, the individual can't develop. That's the essential meaning of the word

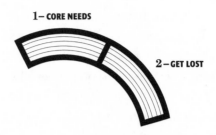

1– CORE NEEDS

2– GET LOST

"lost." Of course, many factors can and do influence the run-up to being "lost": possibly brain chemistry, birth order, gender, genetics, societal influences, sometimes religious formation, luck—lots of things. So go ahead and wade through all the sea of words, conferences, theories, articles, fads. *But understand that beneath them all is the question of the beating heart in need of love and belonging.* That's the Secret.

A hundred roads snake out from the cancer of an unfed heart. There are *many* dead ends and wrong turns that can get us lost, but there's just one way to return home.

My first union job was working construction at age sixteen. As the son of a plasterer, I'd been tending plasterers and bricklayers for a few years before that. So my father put in a good word with a friend of his who owned a construction company. Presto! At sixteen I was hired to tend bricklayers working on a large hospital. One day I was told to go down into this huge basement room to fetch a tool of some kind. The unfinished room was totally dark. I recall being very hesitant about going in there, but I knew better than to say no on the job. So I propped the door open and in I went. Just as I'd feared, a gust of wind slammed the door shut behind me. There I was, totally wrapped in absolute darkness. *Absolute!* I recall holding my hand an inch in front of my face and marveling that I could not see it. Fighting panic, I tried to figure how I could get out of there. I reasoned that if I just walked in a straight line, sooner or later I'd find a wall. Then I'd follow the wall around, and I'd eventually come to a door. Wouldn't I? After all, I wasn't stuck in the Sahara Desert; it was just a room! But the dark was totally disorienting. I couldn't tell if I was going in a straight line or not. For all I knew I was wandering in circles. For the first time in my life, I felt totally lost. I remember sitting down when the darkness just felt too heavy. The longer I sat, the more lost I felt. Time blurred. How long was long? How long had I been in the room? How long had I sat there? No way I could tell.

Since that was some fifty years ago and I'm not still there, I obviously got out. I can't remember how. Probably I just blundered around until by chance I hit a wall.

This is what "lost" is—whether in that pitch black room or lost in the Hoop called life. Lost means not knowing where you are or where you are headed. It means confusion and self-doubt. Lost is the inability to recognize options. Lost means sitting alone in the dark because there isn't a scrap of light anywhere to follow.

The destructive behavior of the lost belies the fact that almost always the outside does not match the inside. If you could see inside the out-of-control person, no matter what the individual looks like on the outside, you'd be looking at a scared, lonely, sad, pissed-off kid who got blown off course and became lost. Sometimes it's terribly hard to see past the bluster, but what you are ultimately looking at is someone stumbling around in absolute darkness.

Get Hurt

Once we get lost, we get hurt. After stumbling around in that dark place for a while, I guess that's no great surprise. Count the ways. Since we are a body-mind-emotions continuum, all this hopeless

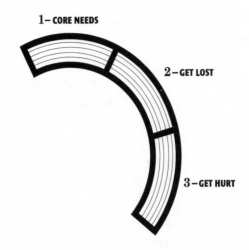

1 – CORE NEEDS

2 – GET LOST

3 – GET HURT

flailing around will affect the body. Before long the emotional trauma finds the body's weakest point to attack: ulcers, cardiovascular damage, depression of various kinds, chronic aches and pains, to name just a few.

Try this: tell me what habitually hurts anyone you are working with and follow your hoop backward. As I said, lots of factors exert influence, but ultimately what you'll discover in the healing process is someone who has learned to crawl out of the darkness to that core that is at the heart of us all.

I see that I won't be able to finish this section tonight; I'm running out of gas, my friend. That happens when you reach the hilltop and are on your way down—at least to me. On the one hand you simply don't have the stamina to do as much as you once did. But on the other, you've gotten smart enough to stop when enough is enough.

But before I close out the day, I want to introduce you to a friend of mine. For quite a while now she's been patiently waiting her turn to come in and talk with you. Let her tell you about hurt and how it fits the Hoop. Her name is Gracie Rose. I met her maybe fifteen years ago, but I haven't seen her for ten years or so.

So I don't know if she ever did make it out of the darkness; I pray she did.

Physically, Gracie was a beautiful girl (talk about a double-edged sword!) and about twenty years old when I knew her. Gracie loved to shock. She showed off her tattoos, chewed tobacco, drove like a maniac, knew how to flaunt her beauty in a way that said, "I know you like what you see. Well, eat your heart out because I'm just playing with you." Sadly, most of who she was hated her body with a passion. On the one hand, she used her body like a flag waving from the rubble of a bombed-out building, begging to be noticed. On the other, she detested ever being seen. She switched her clothes back and forth from tent-like shirts and sweaters to bodysuits so tight you could tell if the dime in her pocket was heads or tails.

Besides trying to deal with her chemical dependency, Gracie was anorexic-bulimic. For more than seven years she'd been riding that roller coaster of death. An evil witch lived in her mirror. As beautiful as she was, honest to God, when she looked in a mirror, she told me that all she saw was a fat, ugly person unworthy of acceptance. Like so many millions of others, she'd been kidnapped off her island and had no idea of how to get back home.

Gracie Rose's grandparents on both sides were nonrecovering alcoholics. From what I could gather, her mother, although not alcoholic, was totally incapable of bonding with her daughter. But considering where that woman had come from, how could she? Long ago she'd been kidnapped herself. She couldn't give what she didn't have.

Gracie Rose had grit going for her. Unlikely as it seems, she managed to squeeze through college by bluff, con, determination—and hard work when she had to. As lost as she was, she was determined to prove to her mother that she was worth something.

In Gracie's four years of college, not once did her mother visit or even call her. Gracie told me that she'd begged her mother to just take her phone number. At least then she could dream that her mother might call. But she never took the number. Inside Gracie Rose, behind all the tobacco juice, tattoos, and attitude was a hopeful little girl wanting so badly for her mom just to give her a call.

Not typically, Gracie Rose had a quasi-decent relationship with her father. After her parents' divorce, any sense of home or family she had, or *ever* had, was with her violent brother and father. It was probably better than nothing, but it wasn't much of an island to stand on.

Once Gracie very proudly showed me a letter her father had written to her. He'd signed it "La La Lo." I asked her what that meant. Embarrassed, she said that as a small girl, she couldn't pronounce "I love you." It came out "La la lo." So for Gracie, through all the dark years, *La La Lo* became a symbol that maybe there was a tiny spark of light somewhere in the universe.

I remember our talks about the witch in Gracie's mirror. I asked her if there was any part of her, even a tiny island of sanity, that could see behind the evil spell. I urged her to try harder. Surely she could see that she was not a deformed creature who deserved nothing better than excommunication from life's banquet. All she had to do was look! Did she *ever* see through the ugly smoke of her abduction from home to get a glimpse of the person everyone else could see?

Fascinating, fascinating! Gracie said that sometimes she could. Sometimes there emerged a tiny part of her that she could stand on, like a postage-stamp-size speck of land in an ocean. In those moments, the way lightning momentarily lights up the sky, she could see that the image of a deformed, fat, ugly girl was false. But these flashes of insight never lasted. The lies were much stronger than the truth. When she could find her way back to that island, however, she knew what it was called. It was a place called *La La Lo.*

I once got a card from her. Can you understand how thrilled I was, my friend? She signed it "La La Lo."

Stop for a moment now. Sit before your open door and watch the parade going by. Invite truth to come sit at your table. Dwell with these people, these angels, that I've introduced to you, and follow the thread. Blow away the accidentals and incidentals about their stories; look to the essence. Can you see that they are all the same story? The same energy. The same Dance. It's all about the same thing—wounding and healing. It's always about being lost and finding your way home. And home is always that tiny island called La La Lo.

When we are kidnapped from our core, we lose more than our ability to love and accept love from others. The primary damage is the loss of our ability to love ourselves. The loss of self-love is the real witch in the mirror. When love is denied, there is an absence, sometimes nearly total, of self-compassion. That's the wound at the core of our being! That bite torn from our souls is the wound that hurts. It devastates. We desperately try to cope, to cover up, each of us according to our different personalities. Count the ways: cynicism, apathy, depression. We embrace eating disorders, addictions, and obsessive-compulsive behavior of all kinds. Some of us flail around in numerous failed relationships as we try to smother the pain. Some of us make idols of material success and others define ourselves by failure. All are the faces of the same loss and hopelessness.

Right here on this hoop is every book ever written on dysfunction, codependency, shame, low self-esteem. Here is the foundation beneath all the works on spiritual immaturity or the quest for self-actualization. Here is the core one must get to if there is to be any lasting change in the quality of our relationships, whether with ourselves, family, a romantic other, God, society, or whomever. There are a thousand models out there and even more ways to improve the quality of life. All good. But in spite of that they are all just sticks thrown into the River. It is *the River* you must come to recognize, my friend. That River itself is our restlessly ongoing effort to be found and so to find or rediscover what we were all made for.

get stuck

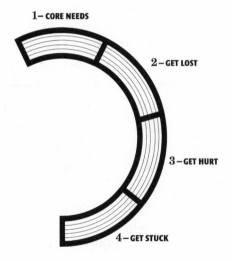

1– CORE NEEDS

2 – GET LOST

3 – GET HURT

4 – GET STUCK

I ask your patience, my friend. Part of me says, "Shorten this up. You're talking too much." Then I answer, "The hell I will. This is my story, and I'll tell it as it comes to me." Long or short, I hope you can follow along my path of breadcrumbs.

Follow the Hoop and see what happens next. We get stuck. It's like what happened to me in that dark room. Options evaporate. People on the outside might shout, "Just get up and get on with it!" All of us are very quick to say how easy it should be for others to get up and get going. "Stuck" means we go on practicing the hurt generated by being lost. Before long, "stuck" becomes the only way we know how to function. Every once in a while there might be a glimmer of light, as Gracie Rose mentioned. But mostly we get good and fixated in the systems that dictate life as we know it. As irrationality becomes normal, one loss leads to another.

There's big time wisdom in understanding how this works. From the outside we don't see the same world the people inside see as they look out. Every living human being wears an emotional lens over their core. As the Koran says, we don't see the world the way it is, we see the world the way *we* are. The more damaged our core, the more damaged the world we can see. How could it be otherwise? If you want to understand why people do some of the tragic, destructive things they do, try looking at the world from their vantage point. Like you, they can only react to the world as they see it. There are no exceptions. Patterns feed on patterns. Systems create like systems. Pretty soon the coping technique we developed to deal with the trauma of being lost hardens into "reality." For us, it *is* reality—not the only reality possible, but the only one available under present circumstances.

Imagine standing next to the Grand Canyon with the Colorado River roaring far below. Eons of weathering have carved that massive canyon. Next to that great chasm, imagine yourself drawing a tiny channel with a stick. Let the river flow; where will it go? What divide will it follow? Even if it "makes sense" for the river to flow along your new, shallow channel, where will the pressure of habit push the life force?

Healing is a tough process, my friend. It really is. Lacking self-compassion, it is next to impossible to get anyone, including ourselves, to even acknowledge our own efforts. It's nothing less than heroic work.

Oops! I thought I told the office to hold my calls since I was going to be concentrating on these pages. Guess I didn't. Anyway, I was informed that I had a call waiting on line two. Fussing and fuming, I took it.

See—wrong again! Such an attitude violates the principles of the Dance. It suggests that my plan is better than The Plan. Instead of "just showing up," I'm trying to take control by conducting the music. As it happened, I needed to listen to the woman making the call. I needed what she had to tell me so I could validate what I'm trying to say to you.

I have no idea who this woman is. She didn't give her name or even say where she was calling from. All I know is that it was a long-distance call. Having tracked me down through the publisher of one of my books, she said, "You sound like someone I can talk to." That's how the Dance works.

Coming from an alcoholic family, she said she'd spent considerable time in a convent. Now in her fifties, she is a part-time schoolteacher, totally alienated from her family. In fact, she's very much isolated from everyone. Part of her version of hurt is the inability to throw anything away. Oddly enough, for her, it's a form of coping. Apparently her apartment is so crammed with stuff there is hardly room to move around. Her garage is in the same shape. With her living space so cluttered, there is almost no room for her to take care of her clothes, personal hygiene, or even to eat. Her surroundings reflect her soul. As her soul was wounded, so are her surroundings.

Her money is almost gone, and her landlord is demanding rent. At one point, she said she'd had plumbing problems. But she was too embarrassed to have anyone in to fix it so she just turned the water off and got what she needed from a gas station on the corner. Making friends is out of the question. What if they wanted to come over?

Her story went on and on, getting worse all the time. How could it not? She is miserable, depressed, lonely to the point of agony, and quickly getting desperate enough to—I hope—make a move. She has been living this way for many years.

This is "stuck." It would be easy to shoot her quick, obvious answers: "Clean the damn place up!" Just as it would be easy to shout at Gracie Rose, "Start eating! You're killing yourself!" But more often than not, to do so makes the possibility of healing all the more remote. Those who give answers like these have no idea of how the Hoop works. They don't get what the root problem is. And if you don't get what the root problem is, how can there ever be a root healing? *Of course* the woman needs to clean up her surroundings, and Gracie Rose needs nourishment! But those things aren't going to happen unless and until that woman begins to understand how to clean up her inner surroundings, and Gracie gets a glimmer of the deeper hunger that is slowly killing her.

Stuck means *can't move.* "Emotional superglue" may be too cute a phrase, but this is a real, most agonizing phase of the Hoop. We get hurt and then we get stuck. The dynamics of stuck invade our innermost parts and become familiar. Whether it's being abused in a relationship, dying around food in one way or another, filling our bodies with drugs, shutting down all feelings, surrendering to violent rage, or isolating or hiding. These behaviors become our pimps, so to speak, and we jump when they beckon.

From the outside, it is so hard to understand. "Why would they put up with that?" or "Why don't they just stop what they're doing?" The answer is because *stuck* is *stuck.* This is not pattycake. As love is our deepest need, the witch in the mirror fosters denial, and the patterns we then spin from that denial are enormously strong. Are you determined to be a "change agent" who invites others to get unstuck? Then know well what you are about. Know what *stuck* means and where its power originates.

Oh, by the way, the telephone caller and I talked about several options, but mostly I told her what a brave, marvelous person she was to have even made the call. I assured her that there were people out there who knew what she was going through and who could and would accept her without judgment. I told her to look for these people. I said that in my experience, they're most often found in groups of people whose character has been forged in the white-hot heat of having lost something crucial and then gradually found it again. Only in this forge is the golden beauty of healing crafted. I urged her to gather up her courage once more and seek out such a group. With all my heart hoping that when she got there, she'd find my friend from San Diego, book in hand, heart in place, just waiting for her, as someone had waited for him. She was stuck, but she was beginning to hear the call.

get called

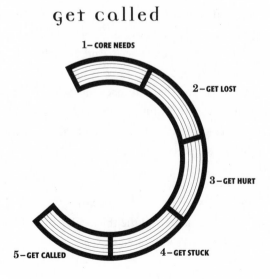

1– CORE NEEDS

2– GET LOST

3– GET HURT

4– GET STUCK

5– GET CALLED

Now let me take you back into the past again. Since starting this project, I've been rummaging through dozens of old journals, letters I saved, poems I'd long ago forgotten, half-fleshed-out short stories or screenplays, character sketches of people hidden in the shadows of memory. Wandering through the cobwebs, I found the following pages marked 1985. I have no idea what was going on or where these words came from, but they capture well this phase of the Hoop, about getting our wake-up call. Oh, yes, there *will* be a wake-up call. How can there be healing if there is not first a call, an invitation to break through all the emotional and intellectual concrete holding us stuck in some anguished expression of diminished life?

> Any knock that invites us to move deeper into our humanity comes from the hand of God. Any invitation to plumb more deeply the meaning of life is the voice of God. The call is often an unexpected light piercing through the dark night. Somehow, instinctively, we see that light leading us somewhere we need to go. A path that is ours and ours alone is illuminated—a path that is specifically for us and known but to ourselves.

> The difficulty, of course, is that that inviting knock is often not of our choosing. In fact, it's usually a call we would not imagine or pick. And even though it beckons us to intimacy, the treasure our hearts so yearn for, we're all too aware that intimacy demands vulnerability— openness to dreadful pain. Even though true intimacy, closeness, and honesty is the sad heart's deepest desire, it is at the same time the heart's greatest fear.

> And what about scars? In no time at all, the sound of the knock that would call us onward is blocked out by our lumpy scar tissue and the thick calluses that have grown over the heart's natural tenderness.

Yet still the knock comes. Again and again and again. Sooner or later, who knows why, after we've successfully defended ourselves from all contact, one invitation is heard through all the scar tissue. A face, a voice, a presence somehow starts to become precious. In spite of our determination to protect ourselves, to *never* allow anyone close enough to hurt us, like a cool breeze on a scorchingly hot day, *we are touched*. Beyond our ability to understand or explain the miracle that it is, like water relentlessly finding a path around all barriers, love happens. Or at least the invitation is received. And now the knock is heard so clearly that it must be acknowledged. A decision has to be made: either the precious new relationship continues or it does not. The call has been heard, the eternal tug of war has been joined.

Who is it that wakes the slumbering heart? Perhaps the call comes in the form of romantic love. For another it may come from a child or a grandchild. For some it is an unlikely friendship that could never have been guessed at. For yet another it may be the discovery of a soul mate, a true kin of the spirit, someone who, seemingly for the first time, understands the true meaning of our words and the ache of our hearts.

The knock has a thousand different faces and forms, yet the invitation is the same. In French it is called *esprit*, yet in any language the meaning is the same: *Even knowing that life is temporary and all relationships are leaves blowing in the wind, this special touching between you and me is unique, and always will be. Between us something of surpassing importance has happened that will forever change me.* Almost any stream can save the life of one who is dying of thirst, yet it is to this, and only this, stream that, at this time, you have found your way. Hearing the call means coming closer to that cool, life-giving water. To respond to the call is to allow that life to touch one's core.

How subtle the call may be! And how subtle the response! So many people see themselves as amateurs at the heart's game, a game they'd lost at before and promised themselves never to play again. Even so, when the call comes, they begin to feel the first soft warmth of hope. More often than not, they begin to think how strange it is to be drawn, after all these years, into a softening of the heart and how much simpler it had been to relegate such encounters to pie in the sky. But it is undeniable when it happens. This call, this voice, this face, this person has touched a place that had been untouched for as long as memory is long. And it is then, when the personal is most profoundly involved, that they begin to know the name of love that is but God's breath among us.

Once the call is heard, it is time to get up!

get up

Get up. To "get up" means just that, you make a start. Getting up doesn't mean all of a sudden you turn into a world-class sprinter. It just means that you are standing up, like a tender blade of new grass, reaching for the sun. If you are a couch potato, your decision to run a marathon doesn't mean that tomorrow you can run the course. It means tomorrow you begin to get in shape so eventually you *can* go the distance. Perhaps it means taking ten steps. Ten steps isn't much, but, by God, it is the most important distance in

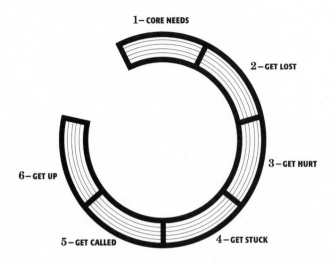

1– CORE NEEDS

2– GET LOST

3– GET HURT

4– GET STUCK

5– GET CALLED

6– GET UP

the whole marathon because it got you going. Getting off the couch is where it all starts. Answering the call is where it all starts.

Put this word in the context of the Hoop: *healing*. Do you see what it means? Here is the most mysterious of all magical moments known to the human experience. Here is conversion, personal redemption, softening of one's heart, a change of direction. Right here at this delicate moment is where God's power is most clearly discernable in human events. The first unstable, wobbly, whispered *yes* after decades—perhaps generations—of *no* is the holy ground on which we stand completely in the presence of God.

Flesh to bone: come with me to a special dance where the precious rhythms of getting up provided the real music. This dance was special because it was held at a chemical-dependency treatment center—the first treatment center I ever worked at. This was back in the early seventies, when treatment was readily available to all. (At least as many people needing treatment are still out there, of course; it's just that treatment isn't as well-funded now—not like it was then.)

What a cast of characters! The first group I was assigned to came right out of Damon Runyan. There was little Mikey who, on top of all his chemical problems, was well into the ravages of multiple sclerosis. But his spirit was as vibrant as his body was wasted. When he got excited in group, he'd start waving his crutches around like helicopter blades. Everyone would scatter when Mikey got going.

Ronnie, big old Ronnie, had raped a date in a Holiday Inn parking lot. He was drunk, of course. It was terrible what he had done, no question. Now the weight of his crime was killing him in return. Many outraged citizens would say, "Castrate the bastard and let him bleed to death in the street!" But I assure you that he was doing a good job of killing himself.

Maurice, gentle Maurice, had tried to shoot himself in the head and missed. At least he missed in terms of the wound not being fatal. But he had succeeded in blowing part of his jaw off. Maurice wore a huge bandage that covered his whole head and one eye. He couldn't get over the fact that he had even screwed up shooting himself. The hole in his face didn't bother him half as much as knowing that he had failed yet again.

Little Jimmy was not much taller than a barstool and he weighed maybe two hundred pounds. He hardly ever said a word unless someone, like Mikey, jumped him. For some reason Mikey had a special a vision of Jimmy; he could see the person hiding behind that wall of silence. He wanted that person to stand up and take some pride in himself. So Mikey would shout and holler, needle, wave his crutches around, jump up and down, do anything he could to get Jimmy talking.

Bob, an American Indian, sold horses to a glue factory. I had no idea such a profession existed, but that's what he did for a living. Bob would buy old, broken-down horses and take them to a factory that "peeled their hides off like taking off your gloves." Big, rangy, funny Bob.

Tiny looked like a comic-book character. Huge. He sported a shaved head with a tattoo of a devil on his scalp. At least he said it was a devil. The guy who did it was drunk at the time, so the details on the tattoo were very strange. But Tiny liked it. I'm sure he could be hell on wheels when under the influence, but dry and in treatment, he was the mellowest of men. During one group session, when everyone was asked to name an animal they thought described them, Tiny replied, "Winnie the Pooh."

Lots of others came and went. No matter how practiced the bluff and bluster, these were beaten, broken people. When it came to self-esteem, to feeling that they deserved a place at the table, or to believing that they were worth taking half a step for, they were totally lost. The only way any of them knew how to relate to anyone, especially a person of the opposite sex, was through the camouflage of an alcoholic haze.

Did I mention that this was a coed treatment center? It wasn't just the guys who were characters there. Bobbi was part owner of an escort service—fancy name for a hooker factory. An incest victim and very beautiful, Bobbi couldn't imagine anyone, especially a man, who would or could ever be the least interested in her unless sex was the calling card. Like all of the patients there, she had only the vaguest idea of what true friendship might be.

Alice was seventy if she was a day. She came from a farm family where cultural development had stopped around 1930. After she had an accident, her husband told her to drink a lot of blackberry brandy to help decrease the pain. Finally, "when things just seemed to keep getting worse," she said she'd had the misfortune of consulting a doctor who could see only a pain-in-the-ass old lady. So he loaded her down with painkillers, which she immediately became addicted to. All her life she'd been isolated on one little farm or another. I'm not sure she even knew what TV was. Then all of a sudden, there she was in a treatment center, sitting next to a guy with the devil tattooed on his bald head. To say that Alice was lost is like saying liquid nitrogen is a bit cold.

Marge was just a good old gal who started drinking with her father because it made her feel accepted by him. For some reason she couldn't understand, she had kept on drinking after the father passed away.

Leslie taught high school, was smart and pretty. I don't remember her story, but she obviously had a problem or she wouldn't have been there with us.

Behind the drinking problem—behind *every* presenting problem—is the greater problem of love hunger. Drying out does nothing to help the love problem. All physical sobriety does is take away the pain reliever. So stripped, the individual must now face the reality of everyday life with the effects of an injured, fearful soul.

Carol was a nurse on that unit. I figured that somehow, somewhere along the line, someone must have stomped on her air hose. Why? Because she had the sensitivity that only comes from having faced death. (Some things you learn only on your knees.) Where those alcoholics were concerned, she saw straight through to the heart of the matter.

It was her idea to sponsor dances. Every so often, maybe once a month, Carol and a few other nurses got permission to decorate the hospital community room and put on an actual dance. Her reasoning was that if treatment was meant to start the healing process, and healing was about learning to respect love, then it only made sense to sponsor a dance in a controlled environment. Regaining lost humanity is always a question of learning to value self, which is always a question of love. And in turn, love is always a question of relationship—not necessarily romantic relationship by any means, but the workings of relationship itself. Because these first steps after getting up are so fragile, so terrifying, didn't it make sense to encourage and protect these halting efforts under the treatment center's umbrella?

Sit very quietly, my friend. Invite the picture of these dances to come to you. Don't hurry. Let the 1970s music swirl around you like mist. Urged by Carol and two fellow nurses, *climb inside* the scene. Maybe it's Carol herself going over to Maurice. People on the street would run away from his mutilated face. Mothers would quickly haul their children to the other side of the street. Even Frankenstein got a better reception! But Carol, seemingly blind to all the shattered scar tissue, inner and outer, leads him out under the five-and-dime streamers of crepe paper. She lets him hold her hand and dance with her. Thus the dance floor becomes sacred ground.

For the first time in her life, Bobbi seems to be learning to laugh and finding good clean fellowship with Bob. Everyone laughed with Bob. Who knows? Maybe Bob, behind the cover of his jokes, was learning as much from Bobbi as she was from him. Could there *possibly* be someone out there who might enjoy being around him just for who he was?

Can you picture Leslie asking Jimmy to dance? I'd bet all the tea in China that a woman had *never* asked Jimmy to dance. Maybe Tiny danced with Alice.

Those dances were not allowed to continue very long. More would have been less, I suppose. But try to picture the scene and fit it into the Hoop.

After the call, there is a getting up, but no one *ever* gets up alone. That isn't the way we are made. Don't misunderstand me, however. There is surely a part of this process that no one can do *but* us. But there is also a major part that we can't do alone. The problem of love hunger simply can't be addressed alone. Love is a "between" kind of thing, meaning that something happens between two poles. One of my favorite sayings of all time comes from Martin Buber: "Love exists between two poles, creating at both ends."

The reality of the healing process is that it's literally too deep for words. I've been thinking of all these "first steps." They occur in so many arenas, in so many different ways!

Yesterday I had a counseling session with a mother and her twenty-year-old daughter. We were sitting at a round table. There were maybe eight inches between the mother's and daughter's hands as they rested on the table. The two of them loved each other very much, yet years and years of scar tissue, grown over hearts of denied love, had kept them apart. Same hoop, same story.

Our session at least got them talking enough so that some contact could be made. But both were extremely hurt and hurtful, needy, untrusting, and untrustworthy. At the end of the session, however, the younger woman, God bless her, inched her fingers across the no man's land and touched her mom's hand. Medals of honor are given to soldiers for less bravery, I think. Beautiful stuff! First steps aren't successful marathons, but they get the ball rolling.

Just think of all the heroic first steps going on out there, walking away from "stuck." It's the real stuff. And behind it all, of course, Schemer is huffing and puffing, prodding and coaxing, maneuvering and plotting to make it happen. As always, the mad puppeteer is hard at work. We are the paints, the canvas is the Hoop.

The bottom-line topic of nearly all these pages is *personal* redemption, *personal* healing. Mostly what I've talked about is the individual's journey down a personal black hole of grief to find joy beyond the hurt. But this is also true: first we make society, then society makes us. It's an allusion to systems.

So let us consider systems—systems that turn the cogs of the wheels of our individuality. Any insight into healing must also address the concept of systems. No one lives in a vacuum. We do not get hurt in a vacuum, nor do we get well in a vacuum.

Systems are networks of relationships that exist for a common purpose. Systems exist to create predictable outcomes. In business, fortunes have been made by creating streamlined systems to produce an efficient outcome. In those cases, the desired outcome is clear—to make more golf balls, computers, or candy bars and to make them more efficiently.

Exactly the same process occurs in other systems whose outcome is not so clearly recognized. When the tree gets bent in a certain manner, for example, the deforming process defends itself, as all habits do. Some systems exist to produce shame, failure, and at-all-costs avoidance of love and acceptance. When those systems are in place, the mind-body-emotions interaction will just clunk away, mercilessly continuing to create the tragic "product" those systems generate—the shriveled soul.

As we are, we train others to be. And others treat us the way we teach them to treat us. Our inner system sets outer systems in motion. Those inner and outer systems mesh together, reinforcing each other to go on producing their outcome.

Those interconnecting systems exist in the larger context of societal systems, religious systems, often extended family systems—all kinds of systems. There are always systems within systems. It is a mistake to see anyone standing alone. None of us do. There are all kinds of forces and powers turning our wheels in predictable, familiar patterns. Perhaps it might look like this:

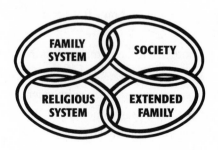

Open the back of a watch. What do you see? The hands do not keep time by accident. Their methodical sweep around the face is *caused*. In the watch's mechanism, one sprocket alone does not keep the hands on course. The desired effect is created by numerous springs, sprockets, jewels—all intermeshing, all acting together for the common purpose.

That is why healing is such heroic work. Changing patterns almost always means throwing a wrench amongst those powerful wheels. *Of course* the wheels resist. The first rule of every system is self-preservation, and systems seek stability. Systems exist for the sake of power. Did you ever know power to relinquish its throne easily?

Case in point: a wealthy grandmother and her two grand-daughters came in to talk. All three of them were trying as hard as they knew how to get along, although all were deeply angry, resentful, turned off.

The grandmother, if you looked at all the systems operating in and around her, knew how to show love only in the act of giving money. It was all that had ever been given her. In fleeting reminiscences, she told of her absent father giving her fabulous presents at birthdays. When I said, "My, you must have been very happy," she told her story. She said she was very lucky to have had the parents she did, but. . . . Then, with that faraway look people often get when they recall long gone days, she added, "There was always a kind of emptiness I could never quite put my finger on." She'd never heard of the "love or love denied" concept. She knew nothing of bent trees growing sideways. But her heart *knew* what I was talking about.

The grandmother had been married four times. Ultimately, each husband was a man who wanted to be taken care of. She had only scorn for those men and for men in general. But she had no idea whatever that there was something in her, some unhealed part, that made her incapable of choosing any but dependent men.

At any rate, she gave as well as she knew how. The grand-daughters, each twenty-something years old, were bound hand and foot to Grandma's checkbook. She paid for their college tuition, cars, clothes, trips. But then the bill collector came. She never let them forget who was paying their way. Do you know what golden handcuffs are? Every communication between them was tainted with humiliating put-downs and comments about the girls not being able to walk around the block without the old woman's help.

For some reason, as I listened to all of this, the first Christmas flashed into my mind. All that the little family wanted was a place in the inn. But what they were offered was a dirty stall out back. Again and again I heard, "There is no room for them in the inn. . . ."

The girls hated their need, hated begging for money. They hated themselves for not walking away and doing without. Other kids made it without such expensive help; why couldn't they? But they wanted the cars and trips more than their integrity. One of the girls said it pretty clearly, "I'm nothing but a whore, Grandma, and you are my john." You can imagine how well that went over.

The grandmother, for her part, sorely resented "being used." Even though she would have it no other way (*knew* no other way), she constantly felt used. And was. "If it weren't for my money, I'd never hear from you kids." Which was true. "If it weren't for your money, maybe you'd treat us with more respect," the girls aid. Which might also have been true.

Systems within systems. Wheels within wheels.

When finally, mercifully, this session ended, I kind of staggered into the hall to get a drink. Sure as hell, after all the spouting off, standing down the hallway about fifty feet ahead of me, there was Granny, shelling out a fistful of bills to the girls. Poison in the giving. Poison in the taking. Gifts as death. No, it's no small thing to change a system.

Hey, here I am at 4:30 A.M. again. This passing the torch business can be hazardous to your health—or at the very least to your sleep! I must be quite a sight sitting here at my typewriter, pressed right up against a dull yellow wall. My little home office is set up off the garage, so I can come out here and bang away without waking anyone up. Slightly to my right is a door with a small window in it facing the back yard. Beyond the window, it's pitch dark. Through a crack under the door I can hear the wind wailing faintly. Eerie. Conjures up the old shaman again throwing his magic powders in the fire.

get going

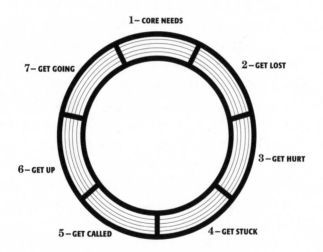

Once we finally get up, once we see the wound and the systems that keep the wound active, the next step is to get going and keep going.

By getting going, I mean just that: get moving and don't stop. That's the trick—keeping it up. Staying at it. An occasional companion on my morning walks says, "It's all practice. Simple as that.

We are what we practice. You want to change something, practice it until you are there." Good stuff.

Once we get started, most of us tend to practice fairly regularly—until the pain of the crisis lessens. Then, frail humans that we are, we stop. And once you stop new movement, it doesn't take long to revert back to stuck. Only it isn't stuck just like it was before. Now it's worse. Now there is the experience of failure, or at least what feels like failure. We tried and failed. The old witch of self-doubt and self-hatred now looms larger. That means the call has to be that much stronger to get us up and on our way again.

I call this phase of the Hoop "working a program." Some people call it "daily disciplines." On my religious path we called it "daily exercises." You can use many models to work a program: twelve-step groups, other recovery programs, body work, yoga, breathing exercises, support groups, art and poetry therapy. Some models focus mainly on nutrition and diet, others on exercise. Some say all you have to do it "act as if." Others say you don't have to do anything but turn it over to God. (Did you ever hear that old story about two farmers who turned their crops over to God? One guy, however, also went out and plowed, planted, weeded, and did the work. The other flopped on the couch to watch TV. . . . Well, you get the point.)

All these methods are good, my friend. All have their place. One size doesn't fit all. At one time a certain discipline may be more appropriate for you than others. But I must caution you that all of them are just sticks in the River.

Don't mistake the sticks for the River. Recognizing the River will help you keep sight of the Hoop. As I said, the Hoop is braided; it wears many faces, the sparks of human existence leap from one phase to another, but it is all there. The story is all there. Whatever model or program you choose for this time in your life, fine. Do it well and do it consistently. But remember that your program is only a harness. It is hitched to the eternal in you, to the spirit that's always eager to return to its point of origin. Along the way you will discover wonders you never dreamed of. You will encounter twists and turns that cannot be anticipated. Your power will come from your openness to learning. As you keep going, your hidden face will gradually emerge. Gradually, you will "earn" your soul—and in time, if you listen well, you will hear a secret name of God known only to you being whispered into your soul. Then it will be yours, in absolute certainty, for all your days.

Flesh to bone. Always flesh to bone.

Here's a letter a woman wrote me several years ago. I assume by now you understand this letter is written *to* me, but it's not really *about* me. I share it to show you the joy and beauty of what happens when someone gets up and gets going. It's how the Hoop works. It's where the Hoop goes, inward and downward. Always inward and downward toward where the tree was bent, then outward into a beautiful flowering of the spirit. God is a crafty one, to be sure. He knows your hidden name, my friend. He knows all our hidden names.

Dear Earnie,

I must tell you of a most wonderful thing that happened to me this week.

I graduated from your Life Management Program in December, and the issue I chose to work on was "repeated problems in relationships." I've been working my program and going to my accountability group faithfully ever since graduation.

Last week was my birthday, and my daughter (age 14) said that she couldn't wait for me to open all my presents. She said I deserved extra presents this year because of all the

changes I had made by going to my Life Management
Program and doing my recovery work. This was from a girl
who ran away from home three times last year.

The note she wrote on my birthday card was so touching
that I cried for joy.

Thank you from the bottom of my heart for creating the
Life Management Program. It has saved my life.

Love,

Penny

chapter 4

Spirituality . . .
I Would Know of God

TIME TO RECORD A FEW THOUGHTS BEFORE HEADING OFF TO WORK, my friend. It makes me laugh: I notice that every time I begin a thought I feel compelled to say, "Now this is really important." But this one *really* is. No kidding.

Sooner or later, if you keep your feet in the Dance, you're going to be forced to figure out your own spirituality, to recast your old ideas. The goal is to arrive at a philosophy that accommodates what you and only you perceive in the Dance.

By spirituality I mean the road, the path through all the incredible, soul-deep events you will touch and taste and hold along the way. What explains it all? What makes sense? In the face of evil and waste so monumental it shreds your soul, when you get knocked down so hard you see stars, where will you find the power to continue? What is the light in your window? Remember that participating in the Dance is like picking up a downed, sparking electrical power line. There's lethal energy at play. Those who would heal pick up the ends of that downed line to allow the power to flow through their beings. That is why it is so dangerous. If you don't have a well-grounded spirituality, a paradigm that allows you to make sense of it, you will not survive. One way or another—there are lots of ways—you just shrivel up and die.

Personally, my friend, I am leery of any so-called spirituality that's not grounded in lived life. There are lots of "spiritualities," mostly based on Eastern views of reality, that are basically retreats from everyday life. I am told that such escapist concepts grew naturally out of centuries of excruciating poverty where life was unbearable for the masses. That makes some sense. In the face of hopeless pain, why not crawl within and never come out?

Such philosophies are bound to be popular. Many of us are all too willing to turn away from the messy inconveniences of the human condition as it seeps through lived life. Life *is* messy. But such turn-away-from-it-all paths are not for healers, at least not as we speak of them. For even though essence always comes before action, the path of the healer leads *off* the mountain, *out* of the cave; it's a *return* from the journey within that leads to that crackling power line and the use of that power and energy for greater healing. In my mind, a journey within that is not validated by a return to the world of people is apt to degenerate into rank selfishness, where the only voice heard is fear talking to itself.

It is a theological fact that we are made in the image of God. And it is a psychological truth that human beings always make God in their own image. The only God people can have is the God of their own understanding. But, of course, God is always beyond our—or any human being's—limited comprehension. Such understanding as there is, however, comes from the complex and baffling juxtaposition of nature and nurture, of our own experiences and the mental and emotional "equipment" those experiences are filtered through. In short, we can only see God through the eyes we have. To a large extent, where we are on the Hoop determines the quality of our vision.

For some, there is the God of the great cathedrals and stained glass windows. There is the God of black robes and powerful, ponderous ritual. There also is the lofty God of academia and the God of certain religious attitudes that are meaner than a rattlesnake. It's not my place or intention to judge any of these faces of God. God will be to each as God is to each.

My God is the god of the Hoop, the God who calls home those lost in darkness. My God is the God of broken hearts and unfulfilled promises. This God knows all about human limitation and frustration and frailty. This is the God of the guy who couldn't shoot well enough to kill himself and the woman dragging herself back into detox after repeated relapses.

I know the God of the three little ladies holding hands at the end of the hall in their senior citizens' home. This God knows all about powerlessness and the fear of losing control of one's coming and going, about weeping when one of your friends is no more. This is the same God who danced with the quasars on the rim of the universe when that convict who had seen and experienced so much darkness decided he wasn't willing to be part of that darkness anymore.

Each of us must come to know our own God. When the line is drawn, I'll take my stand every time with the God of the Hoop, the God of broken hearts who is as busy as only God can be, rescuing the child buried alive within that mountain of stone made of love that never was. I'll stand with the God who understands the need for someone to catch that small body hurtling through the air from the side of the pool, sparkling like a young salmon in the sunshine.

Over the centuries, people have painted God in every color imaginable. The only one I care about is the God locked in mortal combat with "no," the God of the Dance and the Plan behind all our plans. My God is the pulse of energy caught fleetingly out of the corner of the eye—always moving from love denied to love found, from self-destruction to self-compassion.

On the next page is the rest of the Hoop, my friend.

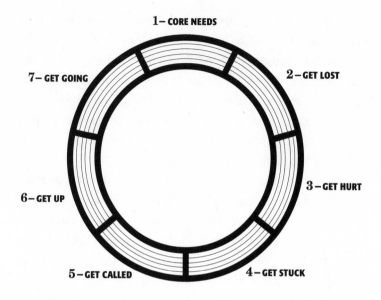

1 – CORE NEEDS
2 – GET LOST
3 – GET HURT
4 – GET STUCK
5 – GET CALLED
6 – GET UP
7 – GET GOING

What seems like a thousand years ago, I complained to an old social worker that a plan I concocted for one of my clients didn't go as I figured it would. He gave me the kind of a look he might have given a mouse trying its luck in a lion's cage. "No shit," he said. I guess he figured it was the only comment the obvious deserved.

*

Are you ready to walk deeper into the mysterious, dark, and beautiful woods, my friend? Let me begin by telling you where this started for me.

Early in 1966, as I told you, I was just starting out. The street was like a two by four that every few hours slammed me in the head. I had come to the party with all my values, perceptions, truths firmly in place—without the slightest awareness of their narrowness. God was good and took care of his own; if you worked hard, you succeeded; nothing existed that could not be changed; everything was a matter of simple choice; people basically got what they deserved, and above all, above all, by God, *I* could make the difference.

Crack cocaine did not exist, then, but there was a lot of heroin. One of those ghosts I spoke of before has just come floating into my mind. She was the first baby I ever saw addicted to dope—a fragile little thing who'd just been born in our third-rate neighborhood hospital. She looked like nothing so much as a little bruise, kind of grape-colored. Shivering. Tiny, tiny little muscles twitching like those of an electrocuted frog. She reminded me of a newborn kitten with eyes not yet open, squeaking for help. For this child there was no help. Who would help her? Her teenage, dope-addict mother? Her hip-hop, long-gone adolescent father? What of her future? Who would ever take care of her? What would ever become of her? Where would she learn love?

I feel the chill of that encounter right now, just as I did then. Some may call it a major learning moment. For me, it was like a tidal wave sweeping away a retaining wall.

What of my tidy formulas? What the hell did this baby ever do to deserve such a miserable start? What choices would she ever have? Just a few years before, her mother had been born in the same condition. How could the life of this little breathing bruise be any different? And what of God? If God was all good and all powerful, how could he allow such waste, such tragedy? If all life is sacred, then how could someone (especially if it is a Someone) stand by and allow this to happen to a human being he supposedly loved? This was a child, for God's sake. A baby! A human being in the process of being thrown out like garbage. How could this happen?

I was stunned. Like candle wax melting into a shapeless blob, I felt my neatly boxed ideas collapsing. My old, cocksure spirituality was not able to sustain a light in the window on this darkest of nights. I was lost. Like any lost soul I had to find a path out. But was it really out? Or was it in? Or was it away? I had no idea. The only thing I knew for sure was that neat boxes no longer sufficed.

About the same time I also began working at a detention center on Sunday afternoons. More than any place else, it was here that my candle melted completely. Part of this detention center was for little kids—toddlers to maybe age six or seven. Baby bruises a few years down the road. On nice days these pint-sized humans, as hungry for love as butterflies for sunlight, were out in the long, grassless yard bounded by an eight-foot cyclone fence. When they saw me coming, they'd run to the fence to peek through the wire. All there is is love and love denied.

Those kids were mostly Black or Hispanic, abandoned or abused. They'd run to the fence and stick their little fingers through the iron triangles as they screamed their names: "I'm Maria, I'm Hector, My name is Jerome. . . ." Pleading as hard as they could for someone to know their names, to recognize them, to take hold of their little fingertips and give them a shake. They wanted so badly just to be touched. Often the boys would take off their shirts, tie them in knots, and try to get a game of catch going back and forth over the eight-foot fence. Anybody to hear them, respond to them, play with them! Or just acknowledge they existed.

At that time I only vaguely had any vision of the acorn in the oak, but whose heart would not ache for such out-of-luck toddlers? As we are bent, so we grow. These are the same kids who would grow up, follow where they were pointed, and eventually victimize not only themselves but also countless others. These adorable, innocent faces begging someone to acknowledge their names would grow into faces society would find far from adorable. Right *here* the wounding was going on that would bleed into all their tomorrows, erupting into unimaginable loss and sorrow. Yet even then I could faintly hear the bargain being forged deep inside them. "Fine, don't hear me now when I have no power. The day will come when I will force you to notice me. We will see who has the power then." We make society. Then society makes us.

But that wasn't my agenda at the time. On those steamy August days the sun was not just baking through my shoes and up my back as I tried to shake fingers, remember names, and play T-shirt catch; it was also cooking away my inner innocence. It was evaporating my simplistic, arrogant spirituality.

Here was a whole field of delicate flowers being sacrificed to public indifference. How could they be abandoned to such a fate? Where would they go? What would become of them? Would anyone ever find them and soften their hearts? What chance did they have for healing?

And God? Again, mostly that. What of God? Was there indeed a God? If so, how could any human look on this scene and still say that God is good? Had I wings, I could have flown over a thousand places and scenes within a few blocks that were just as bereft of sweetness. How could anyone look at the faces through that fence and not question? If I was going to stay there and embrace the Dance, I had to find my path! I had to find a way that made sense, at least for me.

Have you been there yet, my friend? Have you encountered one or many scenes that shake your soul like a pit bull shakes a bone? Have you held a child who's been shot to death or glimpsed the death in the heart of the shooter? Have you attended the funeral of some brave, sweet person gunned down by violence, poverty, loss of hope? Have you been there, my friend? Standing outside your own fence, wondering intensely how to make any kind of sense out of life's failures. At least enough sense to keep the weight of the pain and sorrow from dragging you into a black hole?

If you have, then you know the need to find your path, to discover how you can always keep sight of a light in the window. If you don't, the darkness will crush you.

Enough. Before I end this for tonight, I dug out this poem/stream-of-consciousness rambling from an old journal. Can you hear it?

Oh, God
Have you forsaken us?
The wolves are everywhere.
Devouring the lambs.
Are the lambs
Not yours,
Dear to your heart?
Are you not
All Powerful?
How then do you tolerate such
Slaughter of innocence,
Your beloved?
Where are you?
The doe
Has been dragged down
Predators at her throat.
She cannot rise.
Nor can I.
God, why?
How can such things be?
Have you turned your face
From us?
What
Have we done?

What hope is there
But in you?
If you have left the field
Then hope is
Cruelty.

From my heart to yours, I squeeze out the very essence of what I have learned. What follows is how the path was revealed to me.

I've been sitting at my desk for nearly an hour, listening as I wait before my open door, inviting in whatever truth is wandering about on the other side. The message I'm going to give you is so important! Yet my words can be but a dim expression of my intent. I'll never be able to express to you what I would. But that's okay. That's the point—it's okay. All I can do is the best I can, whether it's putting these feeble words down on paper or attempting to walk with another. The outcome is beyond me. That's the first step on this path I want you to think about—"beyond."

As I have tried to say before, the Dance is beyond. Way, way beyond what we can hope to understand. There are forces at work in the Dance that we can't imagine, but may sometimes glimpse. Every once in a while, if you know what to watch for, you may see a shadow flit by behind what seems like a scene from ordinary life. Coincidence? Fate? A who-would-have-guessed anecdote? After awhile you come to understand it is no such thing. *Everything is connected to everything else.* All energy in humanity is the struggle to return home, back to our core, to La La Lo, in ways beyond anything we could possibly cook up. Life is always struggling to find its way back home.

Beyond our ability to understand random events, you can occasionally see a pattern forming. Teilhard de Chardin called this phenomenon "moving toward Omega Point." In some respects, our participation is hilarious! Many times we bust our hump to do the right thing. We stay up all night figuring, worrying, mulling over just the right words to say. We plan our strategy for an intervention or how to phrase an insight perfectly so *surely* they won't miss it. We cast our line with all the skill at our command. Which is fine. It is our responsibility to do the best we can.

But when all is said and done, after you've done all you know how to do, you may find out later that what made the difference (if you ever find out) was a look on your face you didn't even know was there. Or a word you said that you can't even remember now. One man told me, "What really spoke to me was the slope of your shoulders when you walked out of the room." So much for my brilliant planning!

It's beyond us, way beyond. The Dance isn't about me. It doesn't depend on me or my smarts or my power of persuasion or anything else. (If it does, we are all done for.) It's too much. It's all too much. *The only thing I need to understand is that I don't have to understand.* All I have to do is show up and do as best I can. The rest is out of my hands. Once I understand and accept that, I am at least pointed in the right direction.

But what is this "beyond"? What is the source of this subtle movement of energy from behind the scenes that prods humanity home? And how can it possibly account for bruised babies and tiny fingers reaching through prison wire?

Let me explain as it has been revealed to me.

schemer: the Heart of the Hoop

Maybe you've heard the old saying, "Coincidence is God's way of staying anonymous." But it seems to me that if you look closely, you'll see that coincidence is often God's fingerprint smudging every second of every day. What we so often call coincidence is that mysterious movement of unimaginable energy that is the heart of God dancing us around the Hoop.

Making such monumental coincidence "just happen" *must* be the work of a master schemer—the mad master Schemer who is as far beyond our comprehension as the consciousness of a fly trapped in the cabin of a supersonic jet. What does the fly know of jet propulsion, sonic booms, or how to build a plane? It all looks the same to the fly. He is happily going about his business of persistent pestering, totally unaware of the mechanical marvel transporting him from coast to coast. When the plane lands, he buzzes off into air that is pretty much like the air he left. What does he know of geography or aviation mechanics?

I hear the music of the Dance every time I think about that fly I once saw in a plane. Are we any different? I am as dim as that fly (and that's a putdown to the fly!) insofar as understanding how Schemer goes about his business. God's business, my friend, is the only business of the universe. Life. And the business of all human life is to do its best to fulfill itself.

But here is the rub: there is a paradox buried at the heart of all love. On the one hand, love has but one wish: union. Love is the glue that binds from the inside out. But it's equally true, to the degree that it is genuine, that love sets the beloved free. If love is not free, it is not love. Love that smothers or dominates, that seeks control, may originate from authentic impulses but quickly becomes a deformity. This terrible thing called love not only gives wings to humanity, but it also exposes us humans to a sharply honed sword. Why? *Because love means vulnerability.* After all, in being free, the beloved may say "no." There is no freedom without the ability to say "no," and there is no love without freedom. One who consents to love automatically assumes the very limitations that will break the heart if the beloved refuses to join in the Dance.

＊

It's about an hour later, and I'm snatching at shadows, groping for words. All my thoughts seem as leaden as manhole covers. And this at such an important juncture of our walk!

I do not know how to say this in other than quasi-poetic terms. "Poetic" not because it is other than reality, but because it is hyperreality. This is as real as it gets. That repeated *no* to love weaves its way into the fabric of society and ultimately puts little kids behind prison wires. That *no* is what creates conditions that force Mama Woody to keep a knife up her sleeve. I've seen strong, rational adults crumple like wastepaper in the face of a *no* from their children as they watched the kids walk off into the darkness of drugs. There was nothing they could do but keep a light in the window. How bitter are the tears of all the children who hear *no* from parents who heard only *no* from their own parents stretching back into the endless fog of Jung's collective unconscious.

Why call God "Schemer"? Because we can say no! Saying that may be blasphemy (I only know my own truth), but I believe that even God is limited. Having chosen to define himself to us as love, even God waits at the fence of our freedom as humbly as a zoo animal showing up at feeding time, waiting for us to open the door so we may begin our journey back home. God cannot (I suppose because he *will* not) force *yes*. *Forced love* is an oxymoron. A forced *yes* is an impossible contradiction.

So Schemer is there behind the scenes, furiously nibbling away at our peril, moving pieces around, arranging coincidences, whispering, prompting, urging, inviting, as unnoticed by us as the five-hundred-mile-per-hour thrust of the jet is to the fly. Urging what? The discovery of love. Only in that discovery can the healing begin. Acting as servant to that process of discovery is the healer's way.

Why furiously? Because there is *passion* behind all of this, my friend. What I'm talking about is not a child's game nor just what nice people do. Healing is not a pastime for dilettantes. If you would be part of the healing process that calls life from death, that opens up a heart that has sunk to the bottom of an ocean of petrified tears, you will understand this well enough. When the rock splits and the stone is rolled away, whether in your heart or someone else's, the life that streams out touches the very core of all that is means to be human. Love is *always* passionate.

Consider how passionate and powerful *no* is. Why would *yes* be any less? If anything, I truly believe that God does not mess around. He is as passionate about calling forth *yes* as a loving parent is to find a missing child. Have you seen that, or even watched it on TV? A child is missing. In our age, that always implies the unthinkable horror of abduction. Have you seen the passion in the eyes of the parents? The frantic explosion of energy to do whatever it takes—*anything!* The situation is intolerable. There are no ends to which they will not go. There is nothing they will not attempt. All boundaries are thrown aside. *The child must be found!*

It is with the same intensity that Schemer sets about finding his lost children. But even God will not trespass beyond the wall of our freedom. That is why my clearest concept of God is as Schemer, the mad Schemer. As soon as *no* is heard, he sets a thousand other scenarios in motion, pushing the envelope, but always respecting our freedom. If those plans don't work, others are set in place. If God is love, there can be no other way. Such is the nature of love.

Listen well, my friend. *No* is said as often by those who would be healers as those seeking to be healed. In this world of flesh and blood one of Schemer's main obstacles has to be flesh-and-blood beings. *Us.* If love is the road home, if love is at our core, then how can creatures, who at this stage of development depend so much on the material world, know love but through the material world? An old saint once said, "Nowhere is God closer to humanity than in humanity."

Does this make any sense? Spirituality is joining the Dance! Picture it. Schemer shoving us all over the place, perhaps dressing us up in various costumes to play parts we never could have imagined. Schemer says, "Dance! Let's see if this works. Maybe this will crack a little stone."

That is what Schemer asks of us: "*Let go!* You don't have a clue what I am about. Just show up and let me use you. Just do the best you can and leave the rest to me. Perhaps I'll use you as a vision of strength for someone who needs to know that strength exists. At times, I may use your words, or the look in your eye, or the touch of your hand. Do your best, but understand that although you are as puny as the fly in the plane, that is okay. That is all you have to be. The only thing you must understand is that you don't understand a damn thing. You can't. My ways are complex and mysterious. They're *way* beyond you. But not beyond me. So let go. Let me do *my* thing."

Every healer must find his or her own way. But I can't imagine daring to grab hold of the sparking wire without drawing power from my powerlessness. How can anyone possibly stay in the Dance without that leap of faith into the Beyond? Otherwise the Dance will crush you. For me, that Beyond only makes sense if it is personal. And *personal* only makes sense if it is understood in the context of love. As love dictates freedom, freedom dictates that there are limitations. No matter how badly we want to run back to infancy, when someone else chased away the phantoms of the dark and made everything safe again, in adulthood we learned that is not possible. Adults know all too well that we can lose. There is tragedy. There is loss. People can walk away and not come back. There is unredeemed waste. But this does not mean there is an absence of love. It means that the depth of the pain experienced gives evidence to the depth of the love embraced.

Certainly, it takes a leap of faith. And therein lies the problem. (We will talk more about that later.) How well do you leap? If at *our* core there are major unhealed wounds, giant unattended bite marks, then to that degree we do not, cannot, will not, leap into the Dance of Schemer. Instead we drag anchor by making it *our* dance. We deflect the source of the true power and depend on our own puny power or intelligence or strength. It's as ridiculous as hitching the jumbo jet on the back of the fly and saying, "Take off." Fat chance. How quickly we'll exhaust ourselves, falling flat on the runway without having moved the plane an inch.

It's not our dance, my friend, it's *his*. We are not the Dance, we are just momentary participants. We can be healers only to the extent that we are able to function within these boundaries.

Right now, I pretty much feel like the fly hitched to the plane. I'm exhausted. So I'm going to stop here and wait by my open door to see what Schemer wants to trot out in front of me. I'll be back to paint some more of Schemer's sweet faces for you. Right now, these faces are filling my heart to bursting. As I keep telling you, it is too much—nearly overwhelming. Like everyone else, we need beauty as well as bread. Lucky for us, beauty is everywhere.

But before I go, let me paint this one picture for you. It has to do with passion—not in terms of breathless sex, which is about as deep as our culture goes. I mean passion in the sense of: *I have pitched my tent here and here I will stay. I am here for the duration in the best way I know how to be.* Such passion creates a vision that transforms "ordinary" to "precious." It's the real deal, my friend.

Get your mind around this picture, open your inner ear to the music of the Dance, watch Schemer moving around from the peripheral vision of your soul.

Here's a memory that came back to me as I was looking through an old journal. Despite all the happy paint, the building was clearly an institution. In this case, it was a combination senior citizens' home and a holding station for Alzheimers patients in various stages of decline. Alzheimers or not, human well-being is always about respect, belonging, loving and being loved.

I happened to be there on a special Sunday visiting day—"special" because extra effort was being made to get the "guests" out of the institution for a few hours. Sometimes "out" even included a visit to the place they may or may not remember as home.

As I watched, a long line of residents slowly shuffled off the elevators toward their visitors. Some of their clothes were slightly askew. A few appeared to be totally in a fantasy world; some were like faded movie stars granting audiences to their fans. Others wore the blank stare of utter incomprehension.

Harold must have been in an early stage of slippage. He knew exactly who he was and where he was. At one time he must have been a confident, handsome man. Like a whiff of expensive perfume, a sense of class and dignity still hung around him.

His wife, I don't know her name, anxiously awaited him in the lobby. As he shuffled off the elevator, the light in her eyes shone. To her, in that living space where we all "are," he *was* a movie star. Like a surgeon's scalpel that effortlessly cuts through outward appearances revealing the core, her love did not address the stooped, ill-clothed, shuffling man. Her words said exactly what she felt. "Oh, here comes the king of the mountain!" she exclaimed. For her, this was no mere illusion for the sake of comfort. To her, he was and always would be the king of the mountain.

Her healing love simply bypassed Harold's outward appearance. Such is the Secret. She gave respect, support, encouragement, and acceptance in abundance. No doubt the "king's" air of dignity had relied on that vision for many years. Love creates the vision of the soul.

I was reminded of a great truth tonight, my friend. For the last several hours I sat talking with a fifty-seven-year-old man. He has two children out of college, two still in high school, a wife, a mortgage, and a car payment. In short, he has a middle-class lifestyle. But now he has been "let go" from his job. In the name of "prudent downsizing," his company simply dismissed him after twenty-three years of service. He has skills, certainly, but so do a lot of younger, less expensive, men, who are competing for disappearing positions. He and his wife have little savings since a good chunk of their resources went toward their kids' education. It's not exaggerating to say that the limb of the tree has been cut off behind his perch.

Surprisingly, by the end of our talk, it was almost as if he was reassuring *me* that he would be okay.

"I've been through worse than this and come out on my feet," he said with a brave smile. "Maybe this is the silver lining of having survived tough times."

The great truth: belief is easy; it is *trust* that's hard. Why? Belief is making a promise, but trust is keeping it. Belief says, "Yes, I affirm that if I jump out of this fortieth floor window I will sprout wings and fly up, not fall down." Belief is the thought. Trust is the jumping. Trust is the deed.

The point, my friend, is that freedom, the quest for the Lord of the Hoop, inevitably leads to the other side of trust. Or through the door that is trust. Did not Jesus say something like, "Anyone can say Lord, Lord. It is the one who does the will of God who is justified"?

Because it is only proven through vulnerability, trust is the lynchpin of our walk with God. Without vulnerability there is no real trust. Belief costs nothing. Trust costs everything.

It is not difficult to claim trust in God when nothing is on the line. It is possible to speak with the tongue of angels about the glories of one's faith. But *glory* is just another five-letter word until vulnerability has truly been risked. The great Jewish rabbi Abraham Joshua Heschel put it well, "Prayer begins when our power ends."

I suspect my friend who lost his job is on the verge of finding a depth of faith and intimacy with God that he never knew existed. Or maybe not. He did say he was no stranger to hard times. Perhaps he had found his true security apart from outside circumstances a long time ago. It could be that he and trust are old friends.

What strikes me though, in the very wee hours of this very dark night, is what happens to the huge throng of us humans who never learned to trust. Not really. Not with any depth. How many of us have wept tears of blood, only to find that trust in someone we loved was the cruelest traitor of all? If healing is about wounds, and wounds are about love denied, then where else has the stake been driven but through the heart of one's ability to trust?

Think of all the spirits who have appeared as guides to tell you their stories. Consider the wounds. What was damaged? All Gracie Rose ever wanted was for her mother to visit her at college. In four years the woman had not telephoned even once. The oasis of love Gracie needed to stand on in the center of her being was shrunken to the size of a postage stamp. Think of all those whose every breath whispers in one way or another, "All I ever wanted was for you to love me. Why wouldn't you love me? Why did you leave me? Why did you hurt me? I was such a vulnerable, soft spirit, yet you drove your fist into me a thousand times. Why wouldn't you just love me?"

What of them? If trust is truly the golden doorway to genuine intimacy with God, how is that connection to be made when the ability to trust has been damaged, if not destroyed?

It's easy enough to dismiss such a question saying, "God is stronger than any wound. Leave it to God." But that seems a little glib, doesn't it?

Maybe it's just that I have seen so much cruelty, so much arrogant continuation of mean-spirited patterns of living perpetrated in the name of God. There are many who deny or ignore the terrible damage done, as if it never existed. They claim themselves healed by putting on the name of God without ever doing the work of healing. And that means that the part of them stuck in the darkness will never see the light.

God can be anything he wants to be. It is certainly not up to me to limit the way Schemer chooses to work with anyone. It seems to me, however, that more often than not, faith without genuine healing is thin soup offering little nourishment when depth is what's needed. I'll tell you what I've learned. You live with it awhile, then tell me what makes sense to you. I think, in Schemer's plan, that wounds must be healed. I think it is trust and our ability to experience intimacy that are the first victims of love denied. And I think we can only learn to trust by trusting. We can only learn it is safe to open up by doing so and experiencing that there are, indeed, trustworthy people in this world. We can only learn that it is safe to open up by trying again and again to do so and experiencing that there are, indeed, still some trustworthy people in this world, even if the ones we originally trusted aren't.

I think it is words, hands, eyes, arms, and bodies that injure, and it is words, hands, eyes, arms and bodies that heal. I think this is the way of Schemer, the way of the healer. It is people who imprison children behind chain link fences, and it is people, flesh and blood people (sent by Schemer) who come walking down the sidewalk to hold their fingers, call out their names, and play T-shirt catch with them. It is real flesh and blood that is torn, and it is real flesh and blood that binds up that which is in tatters.

I think that elevating the role of people in healing and spirituality diminishes not one speck of the power of God. Rather, it increases tremendously our responsibility for one another in this most important event in all of human existence: the Dance of Healing.

※

God works "through." Grace is "through." Listen to the story of Sandy and her prom. This memory is one of my most precious possessions. I want to give it to you.

Sandy was one of the most beautiful women I've ever known. When I met her many years ago, she was maybe twenty-five and lived in a place called Trevilla, a home for young adults with serious physical handicaps. Some of the young residents had been in car wrecks or suffered spinal cord injuries. Others, like Sandy, were people born with severe structural or muscular deformities.

Sandy was the most twisted, bent up, muscle-constricted person I've ever seen. To touch her was like touching a block of wood. Her shoulders were as knotted as burls on an oak tree. She was always bent double, her upper arms folded against her chest while, from the elbow down, her lower arms angled out sideways. Sandy's fingers were curled as hard as sticks in a permanent claw.

But you should have seen her eyes! They shone like jewels. Some spirits simply won't be denied. Inside that cage of a body, Sandy was brilliantly alive. She wrote poetry by putting a kind of stick in her mouth and touching the keys of an electric typewriter.

She jiggled and bobbed around a lot, so it was a terrible chore to hit the right key. But I never saw her lose her patience. When she filled up a page she'd have to wait for someone to come along and put a fresh sheet of paper in her machine. Always, she waited with great good humor. Hour after hour she'd sit there writing poems to no one. That always struck me as so sad, writing poems to no one.

Sometimes her poems were about being lonely, but mostly they were about birds or clouds she saw out her window. One was about the sound of a dog barking she could hear at night. Can you believe it? She usually wrote about the *goodness* of life. Once, though, she wrote a poem about never being touched. I recall her saying that it was like a person never getting a drink of water. In the true sense of the word, she was an angel to me, a messenger, and what a message she had! Sandy has long since stepped away into the light.

I used to spend a lot of time at Trevilla, learning what I could, trying to give something back when possible. Much of that time was spent with Sandy. She loved to communicate, especially asking questions about what it must be like to be healthy and young, to go out on dates, to just drive around in a car and go wherever you wanted. One night we talked about something she'd seen in a movie called a "prom." Everyone got dressed up, she said, and the music was very special. The very idea thrilled her.

Well, my friend, I never could dance, and I never felt I was anyone's dream date. But damn! You should have seen the prom we had. I could swear old Schemer even showed up with a tux on! I could just sense his presence all over the place.

Late one night I went up there with a little corsage of carnations and a tape of fifties music. For some reason, Sandy loved the music of that era. Ever hear of a group called the Platters? They're probably all dead now, but they were hot stuff then. One of their great songs (to us at that time) was called, "The Great Pretender."

Well, I got that going on my little two-bit tape player. Then I picked Sandy up (I bet she didn't weigh eighty pounds!) and started to dance. She couldn't put her arms around my neck. The best she could do was to try to put her head on my shoulder. Every once in a while, with a herky-jerky kind of effort, she could flick a gnarled hand and kind of pass it across my cheek. It was the sweetest dance I ever had—a dance within the Dance. Beauty and the Beast. I have no illusions about who Beauty was.

We clomped around for two or three songs. That's all. It wasn't much of a prom, I suppose, but in a way it was glorious beyond words. It was special to her and me. But even then, before I knew much about the Dance or Schemer and his fingerprints, I knew that this was extraordinary. I could almost hear the music behind the music from the tape player. Something else was definitely stirring in that dark room—movement, energy, the fulfillment of some Plan that went far beyond any little plan I could concoct.

Finally, I gave my partner a big, wet one on the forehead and laid her back on her bed. As I gathered up my stuff, she managed to grab my hand. Her eyes were shining softly as she whispered in her croaking voice, "Thank you."

Oh, sweet Jesus! If ever God had a voice, there it was. As clear as the eager hunger of the kids behind the fence, or the twenty-four-karat goodness of Carol and the dances she put on at the treatment center. If you listen, you hear it repeatedly—the Voice, the Dance, Schemer furiously at work. I could feel Sandy tingle when I held and kissed her. How could I ever know what this prom had meant to her? But for complex and subtle reasons I'll never fathom, Schemer said, "She needs to go to a prom. I'm short of a body right now, so you take her." Who was I to decline?

Veteran healers understand this. This perspective is what makes it possible to stay in the Healing Way. Otherwise, it is just too hard. You will have no idea how Schemer is moving you around. So if someone sees you as hero, saint, wise, sunshine, whatever, just accept it. Also accept it if they see you as idiot, bleeding heart, or deluded fool. It's all the same because it isn't about you in the first place. It is about them and Schemer. The wisdom to know that is your spirituality. Be glad you are a player. If people find in you something they need—great!

Understanding these ground rules gives you great power to join in the Dance. If you can accept that you are important to those you would help right now, as the Dance turns, then fine. Use it. Tomorrow, Schemer may have something else in mind. For you and for them. Just show up, my friend. That's all you have to do, just show up. Don't cop out.

Here is another treasure: Imagine a photograph of God. Imagine a photograph of a grandpa and a small boy. See it. They're outside, dressed for a winter's walk.

Have you ever seen anything so perfect? (Nothing like thrusting my perceptions on someone else!)

Try to *read* the picture. See the slant of the bodies, the leaning of one to another. I look at this tiny little person and see a perfect picture of innocence, of trusting dependence.

How well can this little guy take care of himself? What is more helpless than a tiny child? Everything he needs he must get from another. Can he trust those others? Will he ask for bread and be given a scorpion, as the Bible puts it? If so, his lovely little tree will be bent sideways, and so it will grow.

Study the picture. Fat chance a scorpion is going to get in here! Can you read the love? There is nothing within this large person's power that will be denied the child. No protection possible that will be withheld. No advantage that will not be made available. Can you see how special that tiny bundle of humanity is to the larger person? It's La La Lo all over again. It is the solid footing deep in one's core that becomes the foundation that can't be set adrift. What do you think that child could ask for that would be denied?

We cannot out-love God. Whatever love there is between this old man and the tiny child is but a shadow of the love between Schemer and his children. It is total, it is complete. It is unconditional, a dazzlement of delight. The only obstacle is our freedom to say *no*.

However repeated or strong the *no*, Schemer is always out there setting more and more plans in operation and calling out that we may hear, and hearing, find our way home.

I don't know how you could paint a much better picture. Roy, a lovely but scarred man, was telling me about watching his favorite TV show, *Touched by an Angel*. Do you remember it? Two beautiful angels are assigned to help people understand the meaning of life. At the bottom of that meaning is the constant theme *God is love. God loves you.* That's the healer's theme, too.

Anyway, this one episode, Roy told me, was about an old man who was dying. The problem was that his family had a terrible buried secret. The angel's task was to help these family members understand that secret-keeping never produces the peace or safety it seems to offer. The point of the plot was that the secret must be revealed before the man traveled on.

Roy told me how it all worked out. At the end of the show, an angel was leading the old man lovingly, gently through a doorway filled with golden light. They were going home. Before passing into the light, the old man stopped and looked back at his family gathered around his deathbed. The scene was very warm and gentle, Roy said. Obviously, nothing but good things were waiting on the other side of that door.

As Roy told his story, tears streamed down his face. Roy was a man who had been to war. He knew all about standing toe to toe against overwhelming force. No one had ever stepped up to stand beside him. He'd never been led anywhere but to some place where he'd get his head kicked in. That inner part of him that had been so injured over so many years was now weeping. Even though he'd never experienced what it would mean for someone to stand with him, his head told him that such a thing was at least possible. Even if his heart had no knowledge of how sweet this would be, it didn't prevent the longing! With a fierce desire, he desperately hungered for that experience. What could it possibly feel like to have a loving presence lead you to safety?

Roy understood the beauty of the scene he was describing. But could such beauty ever be for *him*? His comment was "When *I* go through that door, I hope someone isn't around the corner waiting to hit me in the face with a shovel."

Many people have never been to La La Lo. What safe place have they ever had to stand on? How could they believe that anything else *could* be possible?

Someday Roy will learn that no one is skulking around the door waiting to attack him with a shovel. But will he have to wait until he dies? Will the icy rock at his core have a chance to melt this side of death?

There are many shades and textures to the reality of healing, the walk of faith. One story can never describe them all. It's always a thrill to hear people talk about changes they have made in their lives. Healing brings the joy of possibilities never thought of until the cycles of destruction were broken. It's the best there is of life, my friend. Not long ago a ponytailed, broken-toothed, hard-as-a-rock young recovering addict put his tiny baby in my arms and said, both defiantly and tearfully, "The cycle stops here."

Whatever answer there is to society's problems, here it is.

That's one face. Here is another.

We were sitting on my favorite bench down by the lake. Fred and I, two middle-aged men just passing the time, but a moment of supreme faith was also taking place. At least for me. Fred had been shot up and down, through many of life's wars. His scars run so deep he was about as blocked from spontaneity and the acceptance of intimacy as a human being can be. But, my God, how he is trying! In his mind, he has seen a light on the other side of the mountain, and he is whole-heartedly committed to getting there. He refuses to be trapped at the level of hurt on the Hoop.

As of yet he has felt no joy. His soul is as cold and hard as a rock in a blizzard. Yet, somehow, at the core of that frozen stone, a deep desire is burning. He has a hunger deeper than all his scars for something better, for that special something that makes us fully human. For the moment, however, he is walking in total darkness. He is reaching for the promise of what *may be,* not celebrating the fulfillment of that promise.

I wish so much, my friend, that you could have seen his eyes and listened to the fierce determination of his words—the *longing!*

"I have no experience yet of what all this seeking is about," he said. "I have yet to taste what I hear others tell me. And I may never . . ."

Then he looked deeply into my eyes. "But I swear that with the last breath I take before I die, I'll still be swinging away with every ounce of strength in my body. I may never get there, but I'll never stop trying."

My eyes filled with tears. "Getting there," of course, is more about letting go and accepting rather than about fighting and swinging. But Fred is striving with every ounce of his being for what Gracie Rose called La La Lo, which is to be found and rescued at last in the arms of healing love. To be sure, there is glory in giving witness when walking in the light. But perhaps the greater glory, the greater faith is to go on struggling against all the scars and hurt when you are still in the dark. I know that God is the God of glory. But sometimes I see his face most clearly—like a miner frantically digging through rock to rescue his mates—as he attacks the rock of people like Fred who have been so terribly hurt, whose scars are so deep yet who refuses to quit. Maybe the sweetest song is not the one that comes from the light, but the voice rising out of the pitch black void saying, "I can't see you, I don't know where you are, but I believe you are there. I am still coming with all my power, on a hope and a prayer. I'm still coming. I will not quit. I will not give up on the Quest."

Maybe it's from the darkness that the greatest statement of faith is sung.

※

Sometimes helping others is a very hands-on project. Two days ago, my friend Mike's son gassed himself in their garage. He was only twenty-four. The family was not religious, so the ceremony will be held at the funeral home instead of at a church. Mike asked me to conduct a short service and to "give the talk."

Usually, when you "give a talk," you are beating the odds if you just do no harm. That doesn't work in this case. At funerals, especially if those who have stepped over are young or have tragically ended their own lives, the emotions are so raw, the questions surrounding the death so inflamed, that you had better do more than just not screw up. When someone is drowning, you sure don't want to just stand there and wave, let alone pull them further under.

It's 1:30 A.M. I can't sleep. The service is in the morning. What to say? What would *you* say? I don't know the answers to all the age old questions of "Why?" or "What if?" or "Should I have done something more?" How do I know? My nerves are vibrating like I'm on a caffeine high. Yesterday, the young man's sister, Kelly, told me that he loved his two cats more than just about anything. In a note he left behind, he told her about the cats. I guess he was giving them to her to care for. So what I am going to do is give this talk as if it is coming from them—a message from Erick's cats. Mostly what I am going to have the cats say is that their kind don't get all tangled up in questions that have no answers. I'm going to have them say that all they are really good at is purring. And for a cat, purring means loving. All there is, all human beings (or cats) can do is to love each other, to purr when another is around. Whether you step across at age twenty-four, fifty-four, or ninety-four, all any of us can do is love. Everything about that other person is out of our control. Ultimately we have no control over other people's decisions, moods, or feelings, or whether they take their medications or not. All we can do is love them.

If you've done that, so say the cats, you've done it all. I'm going to say that cats know nothing of God, so they were of no help on this score. But their impression is that—for our kind—the need to ask questions is both our glory and curse. At times like this, there are always those unanswerable questions about God (unanswerable because they are the wrong questions), like, how could a good God allow such a terrible thing to happen?" Or, what is God trying to teach us by the death of this young man? Those kinds of questions don't have answers, at least, not in my book. Those are trick questions, like how many angels can dance on the head of a pin or can God draw a square circle?

If God is love, then God does not cause terrible things to happen to anyone. God does not even give passive permission to evil.

God does not punish the sins of the father by killing the son. That is not what Scripture means. God does not carry resentments or seek revenge. God is not like a maniacal thief who steals into the house at an unguarded moment to strike down a child.

God doesn't because love doesn't. We are too small to know much of God, but what we can know is perceptible in the reflected light of our own love. In love, as we know it, we see God's reflection most clearly.

Where is God? I'm going to have the mourners move into a meditative state. To hold in their minds and hearts the presence of someone they love at this moment. If they are friends of Erick's, hold him. If they are here to mostly support Mike or his wife, hold them. If they're there for the sister, Kelly, hold her. Surround them with all your compassion, forgiveness, understanding. Hold up in your consciousness what it is you most hope for that person. What do you wish for him or her? Feel that warmth. Wrap yourself in that warmth. Bundle up in it. You want to know where God is? Right there. Touch the love and you are touching God. Look into the face of love and you are looking into the face of God. At least, as best we can know it on this side.

What do you think? Will a message from the cats fly?

Faith has many rewards, my friend. Among them is the conviction that in our sincere effort to court God there will be a breakthrough at some point, though it will probably feel more like a deep breath of cool, sweet air than some frenetic, hard-won discovery. Like walking out of a cold, dark night into the light's warm comfort, you will finally discover God. Not the God of dogma, but the God of life. Such discoveries are not connections of the head, but connections of the heart.

As if meeting a gentle stranger that you somehow immediately trust, you will be powerfully drawn to him. He will pass, effortlessly, beyond all your fears and carefully constructed masks to your heart's deepest desires. He will understand your most private thoughts and personal yearnings. And to your welcome relief, you will know in your deepest heart that *He knows*. Imagine it. You will heave a giant sigh as you let go of prolonged stress. At last, you will surrender, and that surrender will be an entrance, not to defeat but to life's greatest success. For in that release, you will have given yourself permission to be truly and fully known. And somehow, at the side of your glorious new-found companion, you will understand that being fully revealed is not at all about violation, but of completion. The stranger comes to you as a guest, not as a judge. (God, who is love, always comes as a guest.) For the first time, you realize with the amazing clarity that such breakthroughs generate, that it was not the stranger who suddenly appeared—it was you. *You* were the one who finally showed up! It's you who learned to walk in peace, in the cool of the evening, with God.

Between the two of you a deep, mysterious secret, unique in all of creation, will finally have been shared. Now at last, you will know God's hidden name, and he yours. Owning that secret generates true power. At least for now, because now is the limit of your capacity to know. Never again will you walk alone. You will recognize the God that was always there. With new ears you will hear music previously blocked; it's the hymn of the universe swirling around you as ever present as God's arm around your shoulder. You have heard so many people beg in one way or another for the gift of love. Now it is your time, your turn to touch the sweet face of God, so that through you there may be more of light and less of darkness.

Letting Go

A quick snapshot. A woman I saw today said, "It's what you learn after you know it all that counts."

Pretty good. I wonder if she made it up. But, hey—take wisdom wherever you find it. Plenty of wisdom is flying around out there like cosmic dust, free for anyone who's on the lookout for it.

One of life's most remarkable turning points is reached when you find yourself whispering to a parent, "It's okay. You have done enough. It is time to let go."

At that moment, responsibility shifts and a primal torch is passed. A new door to a deeper level opens and somehow, you realize that your life will be different from now on. The life you've called your own has suddenly moved a significant step closer to your own letting go. Seeing the progenitor of your flesh and blood slip away makes the passage onward real and tangible at the level of cells and molecules.

I visited today with a woman of forty who recently gave birth to her first child. She told me in a kind of babbling ecstasy about how the miracle of her new baby had changed her. She was—is—a successful career woman who had never thought much about children. As an animal lover, however, she figured that she basically already knew what all the fuss was about. Now she hastened to tell me how deeply wrong she had been.

One phrase struck me. She was talking about holding her baby up to a mirror. What an experience, she said, to see his perfect, unwrinkled face reflected next to hers, which showed the wear and tear of the years.

"I am an old salmon," she said. "An old salmon who has taken a long, long time to find the stream where I began."

It made her realize deep within that in giving birth she had planted the seed of her ongoing life. Of course, some major new responsibilities were just beginning for her. Yet from the depths of her soul she was saying, "I have done what I was sent here to do."

If life is a hoop, then the beginning and the end are not so far apart. Perhaps greeting new life and saying good-bye to one long lived is only the difference between breath inhaled and that same breath expelled. Yet whatever space exists between start and finish, of this I am sure: as the years speed by, it is only the presence of love in that space that makes any difference at all. It is only love experienced and love yet to be that enables the gentle letting go when one's summons comes.

Human life is prologue. The content of that prologue answers the question, "Prologue to what?" The taste of love is what calls the salmon home to still waters.

I looked deeply into the eyes of my precious four-year-old grandson today and could see backward to the creation of time and forward to the day of my own moving on. Ultimately, life is always about leave-taking. All along the way we shed anchors like dead skin. I love this child with a love that has redefined the world for me; yet, by and by, I will leave him. The only thing that can and does endure is love. The love we plant in others' lives will, mysteriously and over time, sprout and grow in glorious, unrestrained abundance.

Only the legacy of love, passed down, transformed, invested in the lives of others makes it possible to relax when someone whispers to us, "It is okay. You have done enough. It is time to let go."

Then peacefully, silently, the old salmon slips free of constraint, leaving the task of spawning new seeds to others. Then at last we discover the face behind the hand that has been beckoning us home all these years.

I have tried to tell you that the direction of the healing way is always downward, ever deeper. There is no end. As soon as you think you know the meaning of a word, the floor crumbles beneath your feet. *Compassion, courage, hurt, evil, miracle, God*—so many words we have spoken. The tendency is to say, "Oh, yeah, I understand."

Then a deeper level is reached, a greater capacity, and we are able to understand that what we previously saw was but a shadow. This is true not because we are so shallow, but because the reality is so immense.

As far as I have learned, my friend, the ultimate act of a spiritual life is in letting go. So much of our pain is caused by hanging on to our notion of what *must* be (according to us). This controlling attitude negates the Dance. *We are not physical beings having a spiritual experience. We are spiritual beings having a physical experience.* The difference is great. One suggests that we are striving to be what we are not. The other indicates the basic nature of our spiritual selves, making it only natural to let go.

Fear, worry, guilt, hate, resentments, and shame are the poison fruits of the bent tree. Because we are afraid to let go, we desperately hang onto these false saviors. Our weak faith has trouble grasping that there is a loving presence that will catch us. That is why, in my understanding, God must be at the center of the Hoop. We fall inward and downward. Always deeper because God's dwelling place is in our deepest parts. Behind any of these poison fruits is the reality of our hunger for love. Not love as separate *from* us, but love as it expresses itself in and among us.

Our greatest pain comes from not letting go of the fear that stands between us and the light. From isolating ourselves from our own hearts as well as the rest of life. From clamping down and gritting our teeth against the pressure of our wounded inner self that is yearning to be healed. Healing and letting go are synonymous. To be a healer is to provide the net that assures those we would walk with that it is safe to let go. It is safe because I am here to catch you, to walk with you as we both trudge toward the brighter light of the God who lights all our ways.

Think back on all the people you have met so far through these pages. What do they have in common? In spite of all their different walks, each of them finally discovered it was safe to push fear aside and peek out from the shadows. Picture Carol at the treatment center dance, reaching out to touch the man with the hole in his face, or dear Bobbi, daring to risk even the thought that a man could dance with her as a friend and not as a thief.

Think of any of them, of all of them. Many faces, one story. It's all about letting go. Spiritual degeneration is about hanging on.

Again I sit here almost despairing at the inadequacy of these words. They are downright anemic compared to the red-blooded reality of which they speak.

A good friend told me yesterday about running into another of our brothers, a lovely, generous, noble soul who just can't stay sober. Far from not loving or caring, in fact perhaps *because* he feels and cares so much, he just doesn't seem able to let go of all the fears and other agents of destruction that plague his soul. He seems ultimately addicted to the poison fruit of his bent tree. Alcohol medicates his pain.

This man has three children, all grown. Two are actively using chemical dependents. I can't tell you the hours I have spent listening, commiserating, and walking with him as he pondered how to best help his lost children. God, how he loves them! More times than I'd care to count he has suffered through their various treatment-center experiences. Tender and sensitive as he is, he endured hours and hours of "family sessions" with numerous therapists as his kids dumped their rage on him. He was the first to admit that he was far from blameless. Those sessions were absolute hell for him. But he showed up. Now I am told that he is not only drinking again himself, but has also gone out drinking with one of his adult alcoholic daughters.

We either grow enough to let go, or we die. God is at the center of the Hoop, my friend. When we let go, we don't fall down. We rise up into the heart of God.

I heard this great story at an A.A. meeting. A man fell off a cliff, but as he fell he grabbed a branch growing out of the cliff wall. Alas! The weight was too much, and the branch started to come loose. Knowing he was in trouble, the guy called out for help—help from anyone. When no one answered, he decided to give God a try.

Sure enough, the voice of God came over the cliff saying, "You want help, do you? If you're really a believer, I'll help you."

The guy immediately started to bargain, "I'll go to church every Sunday, I'll tithe, give up smoking, and do my best to stop cussing."

"That isn't what it takes," God answered. "Do you *really* believe?"

The branch continued to slip. The man called out louder, "Okay, okay, you are calling the shots! Just tell me what you want."

"Let go of the branch," God replied.

After a minute or so of silence, the man cried out again, "Is anyone else up there?"

That's what it all comes down to.

To know God, let go.

To let go, surrender.

To surrender, accept love.

If you can't, begin to heal.

※

Dipping back into old journals: April 6, 1990.

If I let go
Will I rise up
or will I fall down?
If down
it will be to crash
upon the rocks of chaos.
Surely,
as always before
I will be hurt.
This time perhaps
never to rise.
But if I rise up,
coaxed by my eternal
inner voice,
I shall sprout wings
and pass like an eagle
outward
and inward
to the cool crystal spring
of hidden fiery ice
at my core
where lies my deepest wisdom
and the road
infallibly marked
leads home.
If only,
if only I let go.

I would know of God.
My voice said
know first of faith.
I would know of faith—
my voice said
know first of love.
I would know of love—
my voice said
know first of self.
I would know of self—
my voice said
know first of silence.
I would know of silence—
my voice said
be silent.
I said, "I am afraid."
My voice said
you have begun.

chapter 5

Doing Socrates

"DON'T JUST DO SOMETHING, STAND THERE."

It may seem odd, but I am thinking of Socrates right now. Probably because I am thinking of you. We know that Socrates taught by asking questions, urging his students to reflect on their experiences. And that reminds me of the Buddha who supposedly said, "Don't just do something, stand there." Meaning *think*. Reflect. Examine events to uncover the structure beneath. There you will find the eternal truths and organizing principles that will serve you well.

I've given you the structure of the Hoop as it makes sense to me. Now try it for yourself. What do you see when you review the models of the Hoop, the Bent Tree, the Dance, and the Secret and spirituality? Do you perceive that the Hoop is braided of many-sided stories, all marching to the same music, touching, merging, embracing before flitting away? Or perhaps for now, a few stories are like the unpopular kid at the grade-school dance cowering against the wall, isolating himself from the music. But that isolation, too, is all part of the Dance, all part of the Hoop.

Think about the shadows from the past that have come to speak with you. Consider Mama Woody or Jill, the kids behind the fence in St. Louis, Gracie Rose, Sandy's long ago "prom," or Carol's dance at the treatment center. Now I want to tell you (oh, but it is so much more than just *tell*! I want to paint on the walls of your cave the way Michelangelo painted the Sistine Chapel) some other aspects of the healing Dance as I have experienced it. Then let's walk and talk.

I suppose I could lay out a very tidy, cognitive structure for this part of our discussion. For example, I could (1) start at the beginning of the Hoop and explain each section in the light of these stories. Or maybe (2) illustrate the underlying structure of the Hoop in each segment of these examples. Or better still (3) explain the nature of spirituality in the light of the movement of these snapshots of life.

I could, but I won't. Socrates wouldn't bind a mind like that. I don't know what Schemer will tell you through these stories, but whatever it is I'd like you to tell me what they tell *you*. Try to see them, whatever part reaches out and touches your soul, in the light of some phase of the Hoop. See if you can get beneath the surface.

That's the Secret—recognizing what's beneath the surface. Can you find direction there? For all the variations, tell me about the commonalities of these lives. Explain the unifying principle. Show me the Hoop.

Listen well, my friend. Here are some more guides who have been waiting patiently for their turn.

The monsignor

Monsignor Clem Kern lived in Detroit, where he founded and ran a home for homeless men called Putnam House. One night, in the dead of a winter so cold it could freeze your face, I was with this marvelous healer as he sat next to a poor old fellow who had passed out in the snow and lost most of his fingers to frostbite. On this night Peter had just stumbled into Putnam House. He was still wearing an old, threadbare topcoat, old-fashioned buckled galoshes. Ragged bandages were wrapped around his hands. The monsignor sat next to Peter on the broken couch as casually as if they were sitting in the ritziest club in America. "Would you like a smoke, Peter?" he asked. The old man nodded yes, not sure what this high-ranking cleric was up to. (He was up to healing, that's what.)

So the monsignor pulls out a cigarette, lights it up, takes a couple puffs, then holds it out for the old man to take some drags. Can you feel the healing, the sweetness? Then he reaches again for the cigarette, takes a few puffs and offers his friend another turn, back and forth until they used up the cigarette, which for them in that time and place was a form of Eucharist. By the way, the monsignor, who has long since stepped out of this dim light into brilliant eternity, was a nonsmoker.

Do you understand? Do you see what happened here? Can you tell me what the monsignor knew, what he was doing, and why he did it? That's the Secret. I'd guess that not much later Peter probably died on Detroit's cold streets. But in that moment there was sharing, brotherhood, healing. Essence before action. The Hoop spinning away.

Where on the Hoop do you start? What do you see here? What did the monsignor see that inspired him to offer this Eucharist in the first place? Maybe what will tug at your heart is the likelihood that this homeless old man got that way because of the barbed wire someone had wrapped around his baby flesh. Listen for the whisper and tell me what you hear.

madonna and child

I know a most powerful healer who is a doctor in charge of one of the country's foremost opiate addiction centers. I call him "healer" not because of his medical skills but because of the nature of his spirit. He understands how and why people get hurt. Several years ago he asked me to do an in-service for his staff and patients. His team had developed a new method of detoxing opiate addicts, mostly on crack and heroin, in a matter of days with much less trauma than the usual withdrawal methods. Most of those he served (he clearly saw himself as a servant) were hard-core big-city dwellers, but by no means were they all longtime transients. Many of them, both men and women, had held important jobs. As I sat there in the room with maybe forty of these folks, I took note of the obvious difference between a clean addict and a healed life. Remove the pain reliever of choice from a tormented life and what is left is unmedicated torment.

Many of these folks had long prison records and had perpetrated violence on untold numbers. These were the political footballs that cost society so much and about whom politicians endlessly blather. God only knows how many taxpayers' dollars had gone to servicing the dysfunction in that room!

The doctor had asked me to help with the part of the healing journey that begins *after* drug use. Life after drugs (or any addiction) is the same as life for a nonaddicted person who seeks healing, only exaggerated. If the success of "ordinary life" is defined by the presence of love or love denied, that difference is even more dramatic for these folks.

Of all the stories in that room (actually there was only one story told in different versions) the one that stood out most for me was Angie's. She was there with her eighteen-month-old baby. Madonna and child in a way, but with a difference. Several years ago Angie had sold one of her children to get crack money. Imagine how strong the addiction must have been to break the mother-child bond! But that's what she had done. Now, without her drugs to hide behind, she was trying to rebuild her life in spite of the guilty awareness of this terrible act, among many others.

I asked her if I could hold the baby—such a sweet little weight! Then Angie and I talked while the rest of the meeting went on around us. It was the same story—always the same story—motivating every wounded, self-defeating, soul-killing act. The damage done to her was early, deep, and almost beyond belief. Angie had no core to stand on. But here she was, trying to build where before there was only a kind of doomed emptiness. As the tree is bent. . . . Her final words to me were, "All I ever wanted was to be loved. That is all I ever wanted. Why didn't anyone ever love me?" Everyone in that room said the same thing in one way or another.

So where on the Hoop do we start? What speaks to you? Basic core needs? Maybe you will want to talk about "call" or "being stuck." Maybe the sweeter music of "getting up" or "getting on" is what we will speak of as we walk along. Tell me of the Hoop.

old в l u e

I only knew Blue for about a year. At that time I was a year or so shy of thirty and he was a couple years younger. Blue was already a three-time ex-con when we met at an A.A. club in a Midwestern city. I spent a lot of time there absorbing all the wisdom I could right along with clouds of stale smoke and bad coffee. But that club was a funny place. For all the nitty-gritty, push-and-shove life going on around you, you could still feel angels' wings fluttering.

To say that Blue had been kidnapped from his core would actually be an understatement. His grandmother ran a whorehouse, and though his parents had money, Blue told me, they never took the plastic covers off their new furniture, fearing it might get dirty. Their usual form of discipline for Blue, as a child, was to burn his fingers with matches. Blue didn't think that odd. Like everything else, what any of us gets used to over time is what we know as normal. The first crime Blue could remember being involved in was performing as a lookout for a gang of youths who robbed merchandise from freight trains. He thought he was about five years old then.

As Blue grew through adolescence, his favorite way to operate was robbing what he called "blind pigs." Dope dens, whorehouses, and places where—even if the inhabitants did get robbed—they sure weren't going to call the law. Blue had a special sawed-off shotgun mounted on a swivel and attached to a belt. He'd go in wearing a long coat over his swivel gun. When he got ready, he'd throw back his coat and hit the butt of his gun with the heel of his hand to make it snap up "slick as butter." He liked the weapon on a swivel because "even if you get shot," he explained, "you never drop your gun." Can you see him in your mind's eye? He was one tough, scary hombre.

Yet somewhere down inside, lost as he was, as normal as total chaos seemed to him, he said that what he'd always dreamed about was finding a place that was safe. The last time he went to prison was for murdering a school teacher. He and a friend had been wasting time on a street corner. They wanted to take some girls out, but they didn't have a car. So they sneaked into an apartment building, murdered a teacher they knew, stashed her body in the trunk of her car, and went out on their date. The corpse in the trunk didn't seem to bother anyone too much. Of course, they got caught. Why he wasn't spending the rest of his life in jail I don't know. Maybe because he was so young when it happened. The authorities kept letting him out. He liked "out" better than "in," of course, but said that when he went up the second time it seemed just like going back to the old neighborhood. He already knew most of the guys on his cell block.

When I first met Blue, he had maybe a year's sobriety in the A.A. program. He was busting a gut to point his life in a right direction, thanks to Frank, an old con in prison who'd gotten to him. How he loved Frank! This old timer had told him about sobriety, about how to live, about who was really a winner and who a loser. The time was right. You think Schemer hadn't been dancing a mile a minute to get those two together? There is nothing and no one Schemer can't use to make music at any time. It is beyond anything we can understand!

Blue and I hit it off right away. He was one of the handsomest guys I ever met, kind of like a hardened young Elvis. Since he came from a different world, he had what seemed to me a most bizarre view of everything he saw or did. But different or not, at that point he wanted sobriety and serenity as badly as a human being could want anything.

I remember the day a down-and-out man came in to the A.A. club. He was filthy and of course had no change of clothes. Blue immediately ran home to get some of his own things. But when he got back he said, "We can't give them to him in here. It would hurt his pride. You never want to hurt a guy's pride. Let's go out in the parking lot. He can change out there." Talk about sensitivity! Not bad for a guy who used to carry a swivel gun.

I can't count all the twelve-step calls Blue and I went on. Anytime someone in trouble called for help, we were there. On those calls, he was hell on wheels. As young as he was, he'd been there. That's what I'm trying to tell you—if you've been there, you know. Down deep where foundations are laid, you know. Not that you had to have been in prison or some equally rock-hard place. Everyone has been involved in *life*. "Being there" means you learned, opened up, and came away different. No longer can you keep a low profile on life's radar screen to avoid being hurt, making a mistake, or feeling grief. "Being there" means you allowed yourself to slip beneath the surface of your own deep well and became willing to descend through those frightening dark waters to the source of all that makes you who you are. It means you are willing to gather up all the lost coins that you threw down that well hoping to find the answer. It means you are willing to risk loving, which is to gamble with your soul. As you clutch those lost coins, after awhile you find that the only answer there is, is just showing up every day.

That's all we can do—show up—not knowing where the music of the Dance will take us, certain only that it is to a place we could never imagine. And the step beyond that is knowing that we have no idea what is being played out in the Dance as a whole. Most of the Dance happens in that mysterious dimension of God and life I call *beyond*. I've told you what an angel Mama Woody was to me. I knew her. She didn't know me from dirt, so she didn't realize I was at that meeting that she and Jill attended all those years ago. She never knew that I saw her rusty old knife or Jill's small hand grasping her coat. I'm sure that by now she's put on her golden slippers and is eating honey in the land across the river. So maybe *now* she knows that I am introducing her to you. I don't know. If she's alive on this side, it would probably amaze her right down to her socks. It's always like that, because *most of the Dance takes place outside our field of vision*. That's what makes it possible to stay on the dance floor, *knowing* how much bigger the Dance is than we are. I'll plot and plan the very best I know how, but no big deal. There's a plan in place far greater than my puny plan. God's plan that has room for *no*. Perhaps that's why he huffs and puffs—we all say *no* so often.

Are you following this line of thought, this mental movie? Catch this scene. Blue and I start doing talks together. I was doing a lot more talks in those days because writing books generates access to many speaking engagements. Well, Blue was mostly illiterate. He never wrote any books, but talk about someone who was qualified to say something worth hearing! One of these speaking requests came out of New Orleans. Blue had never been out of his northern state, ". . . except once to Ohio," he said. "We went down there to rob a liquor store." I cleared it with his parole officer, and

Blue was allowed to go with me. The parole officer had some doubts about how safe I'd be traveling with Blue. That made me laugh. I'd been in some pretty dicey situations with Blue by then. Does it seem too sappy, too simple to bring up La La Lo here? But that's what I'm talking about. That's the Secret. By now Blue had experienced a snootfull of La La Lo—part of which was our relationship. He already had showed me a whole lot of what love meant. I was about as lost as he was at that time. We had each found a friend in the other. He knew that I was someone who would never hold his fingers to a match, someone who didn't give a damn if he got the couch dirty or not. I was someone who liked him for who he was. I *wanted* to travel with him, so I went to bat with the authorities on his behalf.

He knew nothing of that before Frank, the fellowship of A.A., our relationship. Bruised babies grow up to be bruised adults. With the best Blue had to give at the time, he told me once with such touching, gentle intensity, "Joe," (for some reason he always called me Joe), "if anyone ever messes with you, you let me know. I'm not good at much, but I can make damn sure that guy never messes with you again." It was the best he had to give. We had a long talk about how that kind of stuff doesn't play anymore, but I can still feel the depth of the gift he offered.

We talked at many big halls filled with kids. I can't tell you all the magnificent work Blue did on that tour. Mostly because I don't know. I don't know how or with whom Schemer used Blue's message. What I do know was that I saw one hell of a warrior out there creating a most unique form of light as only he could. If you ever wanted someone to talk to a young person about what "tough" meant, about the price of stupidity or about whose responsibility it is to straighten up, I don't know how you could find someone better than Blue. He was a man without guile. For all the con in him, when he spoke to your heart, you knew it was coming from some deep authority beyond dispute. Essence before action.

I want to show you a snapshot from our flight down to New Orleans. There were three seats in our row. Blue was at the window, I got the middle seat. On the aisle was a guy in love with his own words. I couldn't shut him up!

My first mistake was to answer his questions about where I was going and why. I didn't introduce Blue because I knew Blue wouldn't want to talk to this man. In Blue's parlance the man was a "normie," a normal guy. Which meant a boring person who didn't know anything. A sack stuffed with empty words.

Pretty soon this guy had plenty to say about the "trash that is ruining our country" and about how prisons have become "country clubs for welfare cheats who won't lift a finger to help themselves." Perversely, his words made me think of Mama Woody trudging up that mean old street with her knife up her sleeve after a long day of scrubbing floors. Beautiful old Mama going to her limit to keep the rats from stealing the cheese from her babies.

As if I was some old crony of his, the man asked what I thought the answer was. I'm sure he thought I'd call for more guns and tougher laws. I was young then, but I'd already learned enough to answer "love." Do you know what I mean by *learned*? Not just in my head. I mean learned in a way that became indelibly imprinted in the soft wax of who I was. Not that then, or now, I could manage to always live there. I couldn't and can't. But I *know* it to be true because my angels showed me: Mama, Gracie Rose, Harold—and Old Blue.

So there was Old Blue sitting right next to me, one seat away from this guy who had not the slightest awareness of the miracle-in-process who was trying as hard as he could to ignore him. That was wise, because Blue didn't deal well with conflict. His negotiating techniques still tended to favor the Smith and Wesson approach.

The man looked at me like I was a simpleton, or worse. I must be one of *them*! And here I was on my way to talk to crowds of people! What if I infected others with such nonsense?

"Too simple," was his final comment. "Love is far too simplistic to be the answer." That about ended our communication.

But he wasn't wholly wrong: love *is* simple. What is infinitely complex is the manner of the Dance. What we can never get a handle on are the endless ways the flowing Energy of Life attempts to draw us back home in spite of all the mud and blood and scars and tears.

Hell yes, I agree that crimes need to be punished. Unfortunately, prisons seem to be a necessity. But they are far from *the* answer. *Our* conversation, my friend, is not about crime, but about healing. They are far different roads.

Stop now and sit before your open door for a while. Invite whatever truth in these words may be there for you to empty itself into your heart.

Each of us must decide our own truth. On the level of basic belief, different people have very different views. You will be surrounded by people with vastly different paradigms than your own. They may ridicule you as a fool and call themselves realists or pragmatists. Most people discount the whole idea of love denied relative to human well-being. What you come to call answers, they will call obstacles. You must decide what *you* believe about what matters. What matters will become your answers. Then you practice those answers. Day in, day out. Pretty soon they become who you are. Every morning when you get up, those answers will be there, part of your vision of life.

Love is by far the most difficult road. Barbed wire and guns are much easier answers. But for the life of me, I'll be darned if I have ever found anything but the paradigm of love and love denied that so directly affects human well-being. Blaming doesn't help. Angie wasn't blaming anyone for her actions. Especially when blaming becomes the last word, it is downright irresponsible. It is a misuse of an important insight. Because, when you think about it, what *haven't* people misused? Misuse of a truth does not invalidate the truth it misrepresents.

What Angie was doing (along with the rest of those heroic folks), was *learning what the problem was* so she could take responsible action. First discovering and then embracing what has been hurt is not the act of an irresponsible coward. It is humanity at its bravest. Either we learn such bravery or society had better continue building forts every second of every day. Perhaps society will never learn that forts don't ensure safety. Why? Because no one is safe if everyone is not safe. Yes, yes, it's a familiar old song, isn't it?

So tell me about Blue. Where do you see him on the Hoop?

sir alex, lord of the dump

No way these pages would be complete without introducing you to Alex. I once had the honor of being part of a memorial event for a glorious healer named Jack Boland. Larry Gatlin of the famous Gatlin Brothers was also at this memorial. He told me that his favorite of the thousands of songs he'd written was "Midnight Choir." It was about a bunch of outcasts from a mission who did most of their living after midnight. If they were the choir, then Alex was the soloist.

I guess you'd say Alex was nondescript. But who ever looks too closely at the homeless? Maybe five foot eight, mostly bald, rather plump, wearing mission-style, grab-bag clothes and walking with a head-down, shuffling gait. But, by God, when you learn to see with new eyes, your focus sharpens. In truth, Alex was anything but ordinary. He had a kind of glow around him, an aura that suggested he had a secret. A bit like Noah working on his boat when everyone else ridiculed him. He didn't care. He knew the rains were coming.

The other person in this story is Sister Kay. I met her at a summer-school session in Chicago. She'd come all the way from New York. Bright as a penny and as committed to healing as Scrooge was to turning a profit. Gentle ferocity.

Talk about the Dance! Long after that summer school, I saw her again. She'd come to visit the city where I lived for a weekend. She had never been here before and never went back again. Alex sure as hell never knew her before and never saw her after. I invited Kay to come down to the mission with me. I wanted to show her where I felt I was getting my real education. Then "it just so happened . . . ." The Dance is always like that—"by accident" or "it just so happened" or "who would have guessed . . . ." Schemer, that's who would have guessed. It was Schemer who ran around behind the scenes planning what no human mind could fathom.

Anyway, it just so happened that Alex was hanging around the mission that day. When he sees us, he scoots over like he's been waiting all day for us to get there. It was as if he had a message to deliver and he'd been wondering what took us so long to show up.

You'd think he was Kay's Ph.D. mentor. After introductions he immediately—even eagerly—asked, "And what is it you do, Sister Kay?" Kay began to tell Sir Alex about all the activities she was involved in, all the ministries and good works. Obviously, she was a woman going all the way in her efforts to leave things better than she found them.

Then very softly and kindly, Alex begins to teach. He tells her not to push so hard. To walk a different road. He says that a good number of years ago his life was a mess—it had been for a long time—until he wandered off into a dump one day. Alex says he was called to that place. He always referred to it as a "dump" because he understood his work there was to leave off, shed like an old snakeskin, all those props he once thought were so necessary. With a twinkle in his eye, like Santa Claus talking to a child, he tells Kay that all her efforts to help people are just twigs in the wind until people go to their own dump. He patted her arm and said, "It don't matter, Kay. Don't matter at all what you do. Nothing changes till people go to the dump and drop off their lies." He was talking about that part of the Hoop I referred to as *getting called.*

Kay laps it up like a kitten going after fresh milk. She knew something special was happening. Alex, her angel this day, tells her that every human being on earth is made for just one thing: to love. That's our evolution, he says. (I didn't realize he even knew the word *evolution*. But then, obviously, there was a lot about Alex that I didn't know.) "With love comes gratitude," he went on. "Nothing good ever happens without gratitude. Love and gratitude. From the womb of gratitude comes compassion. Then he throws in another word: *hospitality*. That was another word I never heard him use before. I guess it was all part of the secret he'd been carrying around inside him.

I still remember his gentleness. He was no fiery-eyed, half-crazed fanatic—just a prophet carrying out his mission. Alex told Kay that almost everyone wastes time and energy chasing meaningless markers of success. The right schools, the right connections, the right investments, marry the right person, have the right kids, join the right country club, and so on. All unimportant, he says. Just like Noah talking to his neighbors before it started to rain, all just meaningless. It's love, he says. Love is success. Love is what we are made for, what we are about. Once we get off that road there is no limit to the misery we can make in our lives. We just walk around full of holes.

Alex patted her arm again and then reached in to touch her soul, "Don't take your work too seriously, Sister Kay. Doesn't mean a thing till people go to their dump."

Then he just got up and walked away like John the Baptist disappearing over the next hill. I guess Kay had been to her dump because she understood. She said she felt as if God had been standing right there talking to her. Perhaps he was. Over the years I've heard a lot of smart people talk about conversion, unexpected learning experiences, moments of grace. I spent a lot of money to take those courses, but I'll be damned if I ever heard it better or more powerfully said than listening to Sir Alex describing his dump. I can't tell you how many times I've used the wisdom of that "chance" encounter over the years.

What is success? What is wisdom? Just last week I was at the bedside of a wonderful woman dying of cancer. She had planted a million seeds of love in her time, yet she still felt sad that her life had not been more successful. Every nickel she ever got she gave to others. Being a grateful Al-Anon member, she never ran out of people in need. So we sat there together and conjured the image of Alex. He came and talked to her spirit just as he had to Kay all those years ago. There is only one success—love. And with love, gratitude, and with gratitude, compassion, and with compassion, hospitality. This lady had it all. She was a highly evolved member of our species. A flower on the stump of humanity.

Come to think of it, there isn't much in all these pages that doesn't reflect Sir Alex, is there? Amazing what you can learn from just hanging around and listening! The last thing Alex said to Kay was, "After all your pushing and shoving is done, just tell the people to love one another. That's all, just love one another."

Guess he had a pretty good secret at that.

What does Alex have to say to you?

The church of saint mickey's

Many people automatically think of church when they think of miracles and grace moments. And thinking about church often involves thoughts of rules, regulations, and dogma. But "church" can be anywhere life is found. For where there is life there is the chance to find love. And where there is love, there is God. Where there is not love, whether it be called a house of God or not, God is not there. One of my favorite churches is a greasy-spoon diner called Mickey's. The following is an excerpt from my journal, written two days before Christmas, 1986.

> I made the time to visit Mickey's yesterday. Why do I so thoroughly enjoy that place? Both the food and the atmosphere are stale and greasy. But to me the place is pure life. Somehow, amid the stained napkins, cigarette-butt-littered floor, loud talk, and tattooed waitresses, when I'm at Mickey's, I just seem to feel the pulse of life pounding away.

> *Grandma*, her shirt proclaims, is the cook this shift. The grill is three feet behind the counter. Grandma is holding court over her spitting-grease hamburgers, potatoes, and omelets. Maybe sixty-five, hair was white as her clicking, slipping false teeth, she knows everyone and has a warm word for all. Just as I entered, a retarded man was getting ready to leave. Calling the fellow by his first name, Elvin, Grandma asked him to sing a Christmas song before she rang him out. He obliged loudly. Rudolph would never have recognized his tune! But behind his Coke-bottle-thick glasses Elvin's eyes were glowing with pleasure at being recognized and asked to sing.

> The busboy/dishwasher/general schlepper was also a large, mentally handicapped man. Grandma kidded him endlessly about being an octopus. Why? Because he needed

so many arms to do his many jobs. It may well be that Grandma herself didn't have a lot of IQ to spare, but she was clearly a genius at playing sweet music on bruised heart strings.

Elvin loudly told the Octopus that someone at the shelter where he was staying had stolen one of his shoes. I looked down and, sure enough, his shoes did not match. Everyone listening made sad noises about his loss, but Elvin himself made no big deal out of it. Such news was just a part of daily life at Mickey's. In contrast, I thought about the huge stink a celebrity radio announcer had made on the air as I was driving down to this diner-church. The announcer's car had been broken into, and he was outraged at the violation of his property! The thieves had gotten away with his radio as well as some Christmas presents he'd left in the back seat. "What is our world coming to?" he kept wailing.

I wondered what he would have said if someone had stolen one of his only pair of shoes. The contrast made me think of the difference between today's Christmas church service with its golden communion plates and well-clothed congregation to the first Christmas in a drafty little cave surrounded by farm animals. As everyone knows, Mary and Joseph were there because no one thought they were worthy to come inside. Because the young couple had so little clout, they ended up staying in a dirty, dark cave. Somehow the congregation at St. Mickey's would understand this kind of thing.

Two young men a few stools over were having an intense discussion about the worst jail to be stuck in. One, the louder of the two, had long blond hair, thick glasses, and a shy smile. He claimed that Fresno was the worst jail he had ever seen. "They kept telling me I had no rights," he said. "Then they told me to look at the ceiling. When I did they smashed my head against the wall. *Mean . . . ,*" he said. "Those guards were real mean."

The other man insisted that Sacramento was the worst. But what he really cared about at that moment was not the relative merits of California jails but the two cookies he had bought, carefully wrapped in paper napkins, and stored in an inside pocket. "Takin' 'em home," he said, "to my family. They like cookies. Got to be sure not to break them."

Grandma's helper was a waitress named Shannon. She was maybe thirty and had thin red hair and badly worn-out shoes. She also wore a Christmas theme sweatshirt and tiny bell earrings she showed off to her customers. Like her mentor she kept up a constant stream of warm banter. She told Elvin he should be on TV. "I've heard a lot worse singers than you on the tube," she said. In no time at all she had him believing that he sounded like Caruso. She told the Octopus she was going to buy him eight watches for Christmas, one for each arm. Both men obviously had a crush on her.

Everyone flourishes in the right environment. Shannon certainly had found hers.

As I always do on my visits to this church, I leave my offering. It's only fair. In this case it was a ten-dollar bill stuck under my plate. Then I hurried out and peeked back in the front window so I could watch Shannon's face when she picked it up. Such a small thing—yet to her, a miracle. From her face you'd think she'd been given a front row seat on the Mount of Transfiguration. I'm sure she has no idea that she was a gift to *me*. I'm not certain exactly what that gift is myself . . . Schemer knows. The Dance goes on.

So what do you see going on in the diner? Where on the Hoop does any of this live? Let's think it over and talk about it later.

All Tommy could do was cry

Remember my friend who was ready to "fire up the Comanche"? The man I prayed you would have the good fortune to ride with? Well here is another one. His name is Tommy; he is also one of my heroes. For more than twenty years he's worked head to head with what he calls "power sex offenders." These are the criminals that many people want capital punishment to avenge. No question they've committed horrible acts. Also no question that there must be consequences for their actions—no matter how badly their tree was bent. Yet somehow Tommy has never lost the ability to see the person behind the crime. He has never lost his sweetness.

Last year he invited me to his facility to give his staff an in-service training. I noticed when I arrived that he was uncharacteristically down, his eyes were red. When I asked him what the problem was he told me that one of his clients, a power sex offender, had a slip from sobriety, got in a car wreck, and died. Tommy wasn't sure if that terrible chain of events was intentional or not.

The point was that he felt so bad about how this one little part of the Dance had ended. "All I could do," he said, "was go in my office, shut the door, and cry. Here was a human being doing the best he could. Then, as far as anyone could tell, it was all over and he didn't make it. It was just sad. He'd been trying so hard."

Adding to Tommy's sadness was the fact that some other staff members seemed not to care, even making jokes about "another predator getting greased."

Tommy just can't understand why or how people in the helping professions could harbor such an attitude. "How can people who are supposedly healers not see the difference between the crime and the criminal? If we can't," he said, "what good are we? Then all we're doing is warehousing criminals." Twenty long years on the job and Tommy has never burned out. Amazing man! He, too, is always ready to "fire up his Comanche."

Envision the Hoop and Schemer at the center. Look at Tommy. Tell me what you see, my friend.

Danny the Night Stalker
This excerpt is from an old journal
dated March 10, 1987

I had a session with Danny today, supposedly to prepare him for his Fifth Step. His face reminded me of a long, scraggly haired Nazi death head. A small, wiry man, he looks like one of the last hippies.

Once Danny got talking, he couldn't stop. I guess it was just his time or for some reason he felt safe. He told me of his countless missions in Vietnam. He was taken into the jungle, always at night, he said, and told to kill everything that lived—man, woman, child, dog, chicken, pig. "Orgies of murder," is what he said it was, out-and-out murder. Even though they called it war, he said he knew somewhere deep inside him that much of what he did was murder. As he spoke, a single tear escaped and ran down his cheek. His voice was as dead as stone, but it was that tear that spoke of the constant war raging within his head as fiercely as any waged in an Asian jungle. Ever since Vietnam, Danny's quality of life had been a casualty of that war.

It was *murder*! What else could it be called?

No matter how you feel about the righteousness of the cause, it's true that this was a man who raised his rifle in concealment, focused the crosshairs, and sent missiles of destruction into muscle, tissue, and bone. And it's also true that within this man was a little boy who squealed in delight when a puppy licked his face, who loved to ride his daddy's shoulders, and was so proud of himself his buttons popped when he learned to tie his shoes and spell his name. Now, however, he saw himself as the nemesis of all living things. You cannot make war on life and win.

There he sat in a chemical-dependency ward, court ordered, soul dead, trying to dampen his boiling emotional lava with drugs and denial. But his soul didn't want to die. Like the tiniest of tracks leading through a monster-infested swamp, that single tear spoke of this grief-crushed man's only hope. To have a chance for redemption, Danny would have to follow that tear back to its origins. Back to the truth imprisoned under all those years of denial. Drugs can be beat, but light can't penetrate denial. Danny must follow that tear track, like Hansel and Gretel followed the trail of bread crumbs, back to his core, even if it's only a speck of solid ground from which he can begin to build a place to live.

How he deserves to live in the light! If only he will. The one tear that leaked away is only a tiny bit of the frozen mountain that somehow melted and managed to escape its brutal warden. Whatever part of him that cared enough to melt even that one tear is still alive. The spirit of the little boy squealing in delight as he plays with his puppy is fighting hard not to disappear forever. Danny is awfully beat up and bruised, woefully scared and abandoned, but hanging tough still. The essence of all that is good in this child-turned-tortured-man is condensed in that single tear. It's there! Life tries so hard to hold onto its spark.

So what do you think? Where on the Hoop do you see Danny? What was the tear all about? Was it the precursor of getting called? How firmly was his tree tied down? Tell me about Danny and the Hoop.

celebrity

"Chance is a nickname for providence."

So said Nicolas de Chamfort, a French writer of the 18th century. How true! The unpredictable is a specialty of Schemer and the Dance. The word "chance" may well be a synonym for *miracle*, because miracles often depend on *when* something happens just as much as *what* happens. If you have a pocket full of cash, spotting a quarter on the street is no big deal. But if you're broke and in desperate need of a quarter to make a phone call, spotting that same quarter seems like a miracle.

Same thing with people. Funny how often it happens that the right person shows up just at the right time. The astounding awareness—when you earn your new eyes—is witnessing the wonder of Schemer pulling on the rope like an Egyptian slave hefting a slab of stone to build the pyramids. That's what's amazing—the all-out, full-blown, just plain dogged commitment of the God I call Schemer. Miracles are but the streetlights glowing green along the highway of the Dance. That's what this section is about—miracles and heroes. After looking at this with your inner eye, you are free, as always, to tell me I'm full of hot air. But first *look!*

I have noticed that God works creatively *through* us to propel us and others to deeper levels on the Hoop. Again, Schemer can use anything and anyone to sing his song of "get up and journey on." Remember that con Frank who talked to Old Blue in prison? Frank may have actually been a pretty terrible person. But that conversation was a birth-point for Blue. Who knows? It may have been the only time Frank *ever* talked like that. I don't know and I don't have to know. All that counts is that the meeting was a door for Blue—and he walked through it.

Heroes are the result of countless birth-points. Think of Ginny answering her twenty-four-hour-a-day hotline. Like their God perhaps, heroes are often distinguished by their doggedness. To be sure, that's a homely virtue. But their doggedness has nothing to do with pursuit of glamour, fame, or the limelight. Their doggedness couldn't be any more counterculture. Maybe that is why they are heroes—or prophets. That's what prophets do, after all. They shout out a challenging message in the face of a disapproving culture. Their lives are the face of Schemer among us.

The word *dogged* makes me think of an old guy I worked construction gangs with as a boy. Bucky Harris was his name. He was a little gnome of a guy, wrinkled, not a tooth in his head.

Bucky liked walnuts. How he could munch on walnuts without teeth was always a mystery to me. If he got a really hard walnut, he'd slide two little pieces of wood way back in his mouth to use as teeth. That's dogged. Dogged and tough. I suspect Bucky didn't think twice about eating walnuts with no teeth. It was hard, but that's just the way it was—life.

My dad once told me a story about Bucky. I don't know if it's true, but it sure makes the point. Apparently he was out walking when a big dog started bothering him. So he kicked the dog. The dog's owner, a burly young guy, started raising hell with Bucky for kicking his dog. Bucky was seventy if he was a day—really old for a laborer. But Bucky was a dogged man. He didn't care. When the young guy shoved Bucky down, he got up and kicked the dog again. It happened over and over. Every time that guy knocked Bucky down, he'd get up and kick the dog. If that guy hadn't got tired of Bucky's foolish game, that old man would still be taking a swipe at the dog every time he got up. Like I said, I'm not sure the story is true, but it sure could be. Some of those weird old guys on the crew were like that.

I've often "gone to school on" offbeat and downright weird people. Yet how often we throw rose petals in front of people who may well not deserve it by half! Society loves celebrity. Like crazed fanatics we automatically give great credence to those who write the books, give the talks, make the flashy infomercials. We respond as if "high profile" equals "deep truth." Even when we know better, the tendency of culture to elevate celebrity is unintelligent, to say the least.

It isn't in the high profile spotlight that true heroics get acted out. The Dance isn't happening up there on the stage, my friend; don't ever think it is. God grabs death by the throat through heroes who live everyday lives. Mostly these fierce battles go unnoticed, unrecognized, especially by the heroes themselves.

This life-saving dedication seems no big deal in the heroes' eyes. It's just life. It's the way it is. Every day you just step up to the plate and take your cuts. Some days you strike out. Some days the pitcher puts the ball right in your ear. No matter. Tomorrow you step up and give it a shot all over again. That's toughness. That's *dogged*.

One year on a long ago construction crew we had a deranged foreman called Screaming Johnny. He *was* his name. One afternoon he pushed a laborer too far. In retaliation this young fellow knocked Johnny down, broke a four-inch tile that splintered like glass, and held one of the shards to Johnny's throat. True to the madness of mobs, everyone on the crew was screaming at the kid to cut Johnny's head off. No one liked him. Luckily, the guy backed off and let Johnny go. I told my dad about the terrifying scene. Laughing, my dad assured me that Johnny didn't care. "Just watch," he said, "Johnny will be back doing the same thing tomorrow. He might be crazy, but he is one tough guy. *Tough* doesn't mean you don't get knocked down. It means you always get up and act the same way as before."

The next day Johnny was his same crazy self. The young guy who had held the razor edge to his throat got himself transferred to another crew.

Now authentic heroes aren't mean like Johnny or simply demented like Bucky. But they get up every day whether they're scared or not, frustrated or not, bored or not, in pain or not—even, and most especially, when it all seems hopeless and they have no idea how it will or could work out. Success is never in the self-glorification or greedy prostitution for worldly success or recognition our culture so worships. Success for heroes means standing upright when all the dust has settled and the spotlight has moved on, standing there and taking your cuts, same as before. *If you want to be the real thing, find those folks and stand in there with them.* Rub up against them, praying that some of what they have may rub off on you so you can pass it on to others.

Celebrities are okay. They have their place. But the best they can do is *talk about* what heroes are *doing.* Virtual reality versus real reality. Listen to your inner voice. It knows the difference between shadow and substance.

scotty and the вishoρ

As I was thinking about all this, a scene from long ago stole into my mind. Remember Scotty, the legless man who charged the gang of punks?

Scotty's castle was called the Arcola Hotel. It was an old, run-down place on the outskirts of lower downtown. Quite recently the city fathers had built a fabulous new convention center not far from the Arcola. Parking wasn't the greatest, so when really big conventions were in town, people would frequently park blocks away and walk to the center. That walk often took them right past the Arcola.

One such big event was a five-state religious-education convention. Thousands upon thousands attended, and celebrities aplenty were there, offering direction and wise counsel. The theme was something like "Bringing Jesus to the streets." I was asked to give one of the talks.

Because I enjoyed hanging around Scotty, I visited him at the Arcola a few hours before my afternoon session was scheduled to start. Scotty's front room looked out directly onto the street, the pilgrims' path to the auditorium. As Scotty and I sat in his room gabbing, every few minutes someone of his kingdom would stop in for direction, advice, or maybe to have the coins in his pocket counted or his shoes tied before he went out. Always with good humor and his rough brand of love, Scotty gave each drop-in visitor a piece of his heart and a boost of self-esteem. This grizzled old fellow, one step from the street himself, was a golden ladder of salvation.

I recall so clearly thinking that it was not I who should be speaking to the assembled throng that day. What did *I* have to say? Here, right *here*, was what all the words were about. Here in the ratty old Arcola was theology and religious education of the purest sort in action.

As I looked out Scotty's window a stream of religion teachers hurried toward the convention center for the afternoon session. At one point a bishop's shiny black car glided by. I had to laugh. If Scotty showed up at the convention center door, he couldn't get in (not that he would want to); he had no ticket. No credentials. Yet looking back on that shabby room I thought about the Arcola's residents, all of them people who'd fallen through the cracks. All they had to do was stick their heads in his door to be crowned with respect and love. What could the bishop, or I, have to say that Scotty wasn't already busy doing?

marge, the nurse from vietnam

Years ago I was trying to express some of the ideas I am writing to you now. What came out then was a kind of play script set in the aftershock of Vietnam. L.C. is one of the main characters; he's dealing with a version of post-traumatic stress. The character of Sunny is, I don't know, maybe God or at least a healer. Their story is about how healing happens, for all of us. (You probably know by now that there are a lot of Vietnams that are nowhere near an

Asian jungle. Hurt is hurt.) I don't know why L.C. starts talking about Marge. Like a lot of these pages, I didn't really write them— they wrote themselves. Mostly I just sit here waiting for the message to move my fingers and watch these words appear on the sheet of paper in front of me.

This section begins well into the play. A lot has happened up to this point, but I think you'll get the drift,

> SUNNY: I give you the gift of caring, L.C., of really car- ing. I will make a safe place for you to come out from under all the hurt that has turned your heart to stone.

> [Deep within L.C. a mystical healing begins. Slowly. Unseen. Sunny's touch has broken through his defensive shield, shoved the gravestone aside, and touched the death of the little boy who once built a shelter for rabbits in his yard so they wouldn't get wet if it rained. The death of a gentle, sensitive, loving little boy who got hurt too often. Sunny's beauty, because she was free to share it, was the cloak this lost child used to protect himself from all the ugliness that deadened his soul. As his sunshine, she was saving his life because she was willing to touch his death. There is no other way to heal the human spirit.]

> L.C.: Two days later I got hit.

> SUNNY: Is that the terrible scar on your back?

> L.C.: Yes. It was a tumbling bullet that went in the front the size of a dime and came out my back the size of a softball. I don't know how it could not have killed me.

> SUNNY: Maybe you were supposed to live before you died.

L.C.: Yeah, maybe. At the hospital in Japan there was this nurse, Marge, who could see past all our terrible wounds. Somehow she saw the souls inside those broken bodies. I loved her, Sunny. Late at night, hours after her shift, she often came back into the ward. That lady really knew what she was doing. It seemed like she heard a voice that no one else did. Somehow she *knew*! Like a real angel, she would walk around carrying comfort and grace from bed to bed.

If a guy had a leg blown off, she would sit and talk to him for a while; then, soft as a shadow, she'd be patting his stump. Somehow she knew he thought himself too ugly to be touched. In fact his greatest fear was that any woman who saw his stump would see him as a freak. Her touch gave him hope.

Another guy got shot in the face. His mouth was gone. The lower part of his face was one big hole. You couldn't see any lips or chin or anything. It was just a blob of exploded skin. Every night Marge would go by his bed, talk to him, and then bend over and kiss that raw hole. She kissed the exact place where his mouth used to be!

His bed was next to mine, so I saw her visits clearly. Every time she left there would be tears on what was left of his face. Somehow, I think she heard him talking to her even though he couldn't make a sound. But she heard what he needed her to know.

SUNNY: Did she give you a gift? [Sunny is mellow. Somehow she perfectly understands what seems mysterious to you. L.C. hesitates.] Did she, L.C.? Did you get a gift? Did Marge ever come looking for you under your mountain of stone?

L.C.: [hesitant] Yes, she did.

SUNNY: Will you tell me? Will you give me that gift? I want to know.

L.C.: I don't know, Sunny. I guess I'm afraid to say it out loud.

SUNNY: I'm right here. Trust me, L.C., trust me.

L.C.: For several nights she stopped by my bed for a few minutes and talked to me. I was relieved that she didn't seem to expect me to talk back. It was more that she was listening, searching, like she was climbing over a wall and looking for a hidden door. I was weak as a kitten and so terribly hurt, my heart and soul far worse than my body.

[He hesitates again.]

SUNNY: L.C.? Please go on and tell me what happened.

[Tears from his eyes]

L.C.: One night, everyone in the ward was asleep or doped out, and Marge shows up. She does her regular routine, talking softly, laughing, holding my hand. Then she says, "Oh, I see you, L.C. I see guilt and shame and a heart paralyzed by too many petrified tears. A heart of stone." Next she presses the back of my hand right up against her breast. For quite a while she just holds it there. "It's okay Mr. Heart-of-Stone," she says. "It really is. You won't die. I promise that you won't die."

I don't think she was talking about physical death. How did she know what was going on inside of me? What was she—a witch or something?

[Sunny is touched. She understands this far better than he. She responds to Marge from deep in her woman's heart. Somehow they, Marge and Sunny, share a secret. Sunny knows. She is there as Healer.]

[After a quiet period]

L.C.: Such a funny thing about Marge. Shortly before I left I felt well enough to walk around. I hadn't seen Marge for weeks. Then, real late one night, I suddenly woke up. I thought I heard a voice—*her* voice calling out to me. Not any physical voice—I just kind of heard her in my heart. [Sunny is resting her head on top of L.C.'s. He can't see her face. She smiles knowingly. She, too, has heard such voices.] I don't know how or why, but I was being called to get moving. I had someplace to go. I was needed. Suddenly I knew there was something important for me to do.

I got up and just started walking. It was raining to beat hell that night, but I knew I had to go outside. Right out the door and around the corner I found Marge in a kind of alley. She was propped up against a wall, drunk. It looked like she had fallen and broken her nose. There was blood all over. "Oh, Stone Man," she cried out. "How nice of you to come get me! I got knocked down and can't get up. Can you help me up?" Then she just starts crying. "I've had enough," she says. "I've seen too much blood and pain and hurt. I don't have room for any more. It has eaten me up until there's nothing left. I have nothing left to give."

For a while we just sat there in the rain. She wouldn't move. Then she threw up, and I just held her. It didn't matter, all the blood and tears and vomit and rain. I just held her and we cried together.

That's the last I saw of her. She rotated out. Her assignment had been only temporary. Isn't that nuts about hearing her voice?

SUNNY: We are all just temporary, L.C. But as we pass by each other we have a chance to create some light before moving on. That's how it is. [She looks into his eyes, lifting his head.] And no, I don't think it is strange about the Voice at all.

Are you with me, my friend? L.C.'s story goes on, but this is enough to give you the idea of it. Maybe I should have provided more structure to help you process these slices of life. I didn't want to do that, though. I want you to follow *your* spirit. Listen to your Voice. What does it tell you? Where does it take you? What is Marge's secret? Why does she do what she does? What does it cost her? Why is it that all healers, sooner or later, "get knocked down so hard they don't think they can get up"? What is that all about? What does it mean, that Marge "was saving his life because she was willing to touch his death"? Will every soul you touch walk away with a piece of your soul?

Let's do Socrates. Let's walk and talk. Tell me of the Hoop.

"molly, i'm your dad"

God painted me another beautiful picture yesterday. I've been contemplating it for a couple of hours. That's the thing with art, especially the art of life unfolding all around us: it takes time in reflection to realize what you've seen.

I had taken my seat for a flight to San Francisco. I was in a two-seat aisle on the outside. So far the inside seat was unoccupied. I was praying to the great god of no-shows that I'd get both seats to myself. No such luck, thanks to Schemer. Just before the doors closed, a man pushed past me into the window seat. It was obvious that he was—or had been—a biker. He had Harley written all over him. He also looked like a guy who had never had an off button. Tattooed hands and arms, bushy beard, and long hair. A big old chain on his wallet. Steel-callused hands with deeply ingrained grease under his nails and in the cracks of his skin. He was carrying a small camcorder which I thought kind of strange. He appeared to be maybe fifty years old.

It wasn't long into the flight before he introduced himself (his name was Archie) and thundered into his story. I guess that good old boy really needed to talk.

He said that, the night before, his daughter had called him. He had not seen her for eighteen years! Then, right out of the blue, he heard her voice. Some two decades earlier Archie had been an outlaw biker married to a beautiful young lady who'd "come from money." For some reason, he said, her folks didn't like him. "I never did nothing to those people," he said. "For the life of me I still can't figure out why they were so down on me."

One day he came back "off the road" (whatever that means), and found that his wife and six-month-old baby daughter were gone. Vanished! Not even a photograph left. Archie said he nearly went wild with grief. And then he headed over to her folks' house, where he wasn't welcome. After the father-in-law had Archie put in jail, he finally figured that road was closed. For many months, Archie said, he'd sit in a park across from her parents' home, just hoping to catch a glimpse of his wife and baby daughter. "Never did, not once," he said. "So what the hell—even the toughest man gets stomped long enough, he's got to back off." So that's what he did. Slowly, slowly, and moving farther and farther away.

Eventually, Archie wound up in Iowa. Before long he owned his own diesel repair company and was doing very well, thank you. Then he married a woman who was also diesel certified. They had two beautiful little girls. "Take a look," he said, holding up his camcorder so I could see for myself. Sure enough. His wife was a petite blond with a ponytail. "She was the only woman with forty-seven men in diesel school," Archie said proudly. "She's tougher than any man I ever met." His daughters were six and eight. Beautiful, beautiful little ladies.

"Then last night," Archie went on, "right out of the blue, my phone rang. A young woman's voice said, 'I'm not sure I have the right person. My name is Molly and I'm looking for . . . .'" With tears running down his creased, leathery cheeks Archie went on, "I stopped her right there and said, 'Molly, I'm your dad.'"

The girl's grandparents had recently passed away. Perhaps that's what gave her the freedom to take up her search. Through the Internet she'd come up with forty-seven men with her dad's name. Molly said she was prepared to call every one of them. But she had struck gold on her third try.

She had just completed her first year of pre-med, Archie reported in absolute awe. She'd called to see if he'd like to meet her. "'Hell, yes,' I told her! Tomorrow!" I said. "I'll be on the damned old plane tomorrow if you'll meet me at the airport."

He had started driving at 2 A.M. to get to Minneapolis, where he purchased the last seat on the first plane out. That was the seat next to me. It was only the second time he had ever flown. He said the ticket cost him nearly a month's pay. "No matter," he said. "Money ain't shit compared to this."

I can't adequately explain how excited he was. The closer we came to touchdown the more nervous he got. "Don't even know if I'll recognize her," he mumbled. I assured him that he would. Molly would be the one with the big, bright sign saying, "I love you, Daddy."

As we swooped in, he started to hyperventilate. Frantically, he started to smooth his hair and beard with his hands. "Got to get my rough old self together," he kept saying. "Got to get my rough old self together." Can you see this in your mind's eye? Isn't it precious? Can you see Schemer blowing in the sails of these two small ships bound around the Hoop?

You can bet I was trailing Archie like a bloodhound as he got off the plane. Sure enough, Molly was a tall, lovely young woman. She wore a navy blue blazer, a pale yellow silk blouse, designer jeans, and expensive looking leather loafers. Her blond hair was pulled back in a ponytail. I thought she looked a bit like Woody's old girlfriend Kelly on the TV show *Cheers*.

Beauty and the Beast? Not at all. That misses all sense of seeing beneath the shallow, mostly misleading surface. It was Beauty and the Beauty.

Father and daughter just stood looking at each other for a few moments while people in a hurry swirled all around them. Then the two lost parts flew together like attracting magnets. Quite a sight. I thought I could hear the faint sound of a flute.

chapter 6

You First

"ONLY WOUNDED SOLDIERS MAY SERVE."

You still with me, partner? Now comes the hard part.
Whether you leave the Dance or hang in there and grow into a
truly powerful participant, here is where it will happen; it starts
with you. What about your *own* healing? You first.

We've spoken much about the Dance, that fundamental core
of La La Lo, and about how Schemer is a passionate God who
constantly creates a homing wind that pursues and pursues and
pursues. Well, my friend, one of those he's after is *you*. You also
are a target. If healing is about returning home, and that journey
is about tending the wounds that hold us back, then our first task
as healers is definitely *not* to heal anyone else. First we must look
to ourselves. As I write and as you read, Schemer is busily hatch-
ing new and better plans to break open our rocky shells.

Three quick reasons why it has to start with you:

1. *You have no right to ask someone to go where you are
   not brave enough to go yourself.* Healing depends on
   our willingness to walk ever deeper into our own
   humanity so we can embrace *both* the light and the
   dark. In all of our lives there comes a time when the
   invitation, the Call, is unmistakable. We are clearly
   being beckoned to go beyond the safety of routine. You
   cannot plan for these invitations, but when they come,

you will know. Your choice then is yes or no. You can refuse the journey. It may well scare the hell out of you. But with every refusal the hinges on the slamming door become rustier. Because your deeper self waits behind that door, you must go forward sooner or later. That's the only way you can grow as healer.

2. *Our power develops in direct proportion to our willingness to be healed.* Not power as force; force means making others do your will. The power I'm talking about is the ability to invite others to become their own best selves. Healing power requires you to take part in Schemer's Dance so that others can catch a glimpse of what is possible. But you can only do that to the extent you have allowed yourself to be healed. The foremost task isn't to help others! Helping others is an offshoot of being willing to search out your own way home.

Remember Jill? She grabbed hold of Mama Woody's coat on her way to take care of business. What good would it do to take hold of the coat of someone who isn't going anywhere? In this case, where we need to be going, to be led, is back to where we started. If you're not sure you understand what I'm saying, wait a while and think about it. Let these words be like seeds planted for a future harvest. The time will come when it will be important for you to return and pick their fruit.

3. *I hope it goes without saying that your unhealed wounds hurt others.* Sincerely wishing to do only good doesn't change that. Your greatest sorrow will come when that part of you that still needs healing causes injury to the very people you are trying to help heal. The medium of your art is your own and others' most tender parts.

Many will lay their unprotected hearts in your hands like baby birds fallen from the nest. Their vulnerability will be total. What "self" will you present? The barbarian at the gate or the protective host? This position is a razor-edged sword for both of you. On the one hand the preciousness of receiving someone's trust is very moving. On the other hand, the opportunity, if not temptation, to exert your power in an unworthy manner is ever present.

BOUNDARIES

What part of *you* remains fixated in hurt and loss, my friend? In that place is the trapdoor that leads to temptation and failure. It's all about boundaries.

Much has been written about boundaries. In my opinion, most of these explanations aren't deep enough because they don't go to the core of the issue. Instead they focus on cognitive recognition of where boundary collapse happens, results and consequences, and so on. It's all good stuff, but wherever there is a boundary issue you can bet the farm there is at core some healing that yet needs to happen. Somewhere down inside is a lost part trying to find its way back home before it hurts itself or others. Being unhealed, this wounded part just doesn't know how to make wise decisions. So it reaches out in ways that don't work: boundary collapse.

One of the coolest would-be healers I ever knew had personality, brains, energy, and a heart as good as gold. But like Danny and Gracie Rose and all the rest something terrible had happened at this man's core long ago. I don't know his whole story, and it's not important right now. The result was that he found himself blocked off from intimacy, stranded on the other side of any chance for bliss. Perhaps it was numbing touch deprivation that hurt him. Because as intelligent and kindly as this man was, he had no feel for the boundaries around appropriate touch. He wasn't a rapist, and he never physically abused anyone. But you could just see the inappropriate longing in his touch whenever he was around women who were vulnerable to him. Inevitably, he finally crossed the line and disappeared down that slippery slope.

None of us, when we were starting out, knew anything about what I'm telling you now. No one mentioned cores or love hunger, La La Lo, or the tragedy that is generated by deep, unhealed wounds. This man didn't have a clue. All he knew was that try as he might, wish as he might, there was a boundary he couldn't manage. All the cognitive behavior modification in the world wasn't strong enough to reign in the wild rush of his pitiful attempts at fulfillment. It destroyed him. In the end this fine man crashed and burned. All the good that he might have done was aborted. If only he'd found his way to healing!

Many healers, perhaps most, go largely unhealed themselves. Have you recognized boundary collapse in other professionals? There are some who can't leave their work at work, some who can't care, and some who turn their hurt to lust for power over those who are too powerless to protect themselves. The faces of severe dysfunction are many—and, sadly, quite familiar.

So how about you, my friend? How about you? Dr. Bob, a cofounder of A.A., had a wise saying: "Trust God, clean house, and help others." Is there a corner of your house that needs cleaning? It isn't a job anyone looks forward to. It's certainly not glamorous. But it is *essential*. So don't avoid your own dark corners. That's where your promise and power reside.

Recently I got this message in a fortune cookie: *Trying only creates impossibilities. Let go to achieve what you desire.* Good stuff. But I've found that it's pretty hard to let go of what you don't know is there.

This is the anniversary of the Mick's death. That's Mickey Mantle, of course. I can hardly believe it! Recent pictures in the media clearly showed him fading away, but my mind somehow blotted out the reality. Back in the day, when he entered the major leagues as a nineteen-year-old, he was the very embodiment of our youth.

Mickey's last media exposure revealed an infinitely sad man, full of remorse at what he considered his wasted talents. About being a role model he said, "I'm not one." Oh, but he was wrong about that! You are for me, Mick. You are for me. The home run you hit with your life was far greater than any boomer you crunched off your bat. How I hope that in a final gasp there was a mighty explosion of self-compassion that allowed you to forgive yourself, an explosion that vaporized all that guilt and regret. If not then, surely now.

When you left, Mick, the world suddenly got a lot older.

I was out at the megamall messing around with the grandkids the other day. We happened by one of those science specialty stores. Right out front was a huge, transparent globe with electricity dancing inside. Have you ever seen one? When you touch the globe a staggering jolt of electricity reaches out from the core to whatever spot you're touching. The kids loved seeing all that red and blue light dancing around their little hands.

To me, the lightning-in-a-globe suggested a metaphor for another truth about taking care of oneself. For years it's been commonly accepted that a human being is a mind-body-spirit entity. You can't damage one part without damaging the whole. Yet we seem to have a hell of a time honoring all three elements. Especially the omnipresence of virtual reality via electronics furthers our confusion about what's real and what's not.

To put it bluntly, too many professionals in the helping fields do a lousy job of self-care. We demand much more of our clients or patients. Why does that happen? Perhaps we get too tired or too busy or too bruised. So why are we so surprised when the bottom begins to fall out of our world?

Think of a big triangle. At each corner see the words *mind, body,* and *spirit.*

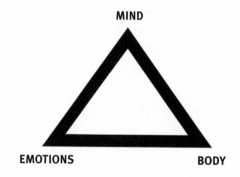

These three are different windows of the same house—all connected. Touch one and you touch them all. How many times has a simple touch had profound effects on emotions? How many times has a relaxing massage or a steamy shower changed our physical well being? How many times has the emotional component of falling in love profoundly influenced the way we think?

It goes the other way, too, of course. Pain, fear, anger, hate—each one affects the whole package. The other day I was out for a walk when I came to a yard surrounded by a slatted fence. Unaware of the dog lurking behind those slats, I was thinking about something else when all of a sudden the beast let out a roar and charged into the fence. No way the dog could have gotten to me through the sturdy fence, but my adrenaline didn't know that! In a flash my heart was pounding, my knees went weak, and my mind shouted "Run!"

How can anyone *not* buy into the concept and the obvious reality of emotions-mind-body unity?

Now draw a second triangle inside the first.

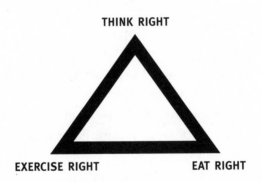

THINK RIGHT

EXERCISE RIGHT   EAT RIGHT

How important is it to care for the integral components that make us one? Every recovery or health program in the world comes down to that inner triangle: *think right, eat right, exercise right.* Around each of those dictums numerous books have been written, new techniques developed, and methodologies evolved over the years. Some approaches focus more on one aspect than another. (At times I suppose we need more focus on one aspect than on another.) But sooner or later, if the whole person isn't brought back into balance, what is good and whole in itself will become exaggerated and thus deform the whole. The most finely tuned athlete in the world can be a spiritual wreck, as can the most intellectually gifted or those who seem to specialize in compulsively taking their emotional temperature.

My point about the globe is that in all we do, think, see, experience, there's a constant jumping around of dancing electricity or energy. The quivering blue light jumps from one corner of the triangle to another. When that dog charged the fence, for example, what system sprang into motion? *All of them.*

Whatever methods and models you espouse, you must learn to take care of yourself. In a whole, balanced aspect, you must learn self-care. Have you gotten started on that?

✷

I sit here reading what I wrote to you earlier. This self-care business sounds like pretty normal, routine stuff, doesn't it? Or does it? Take another step with me down into the rabbit hole.

I'm not sure how to say this, but maybe you can get my meaning by reading between the lines: *all the self-care in the world doesn't necessarily indicate a willingness to journey within.* Are you willing to sink beneath the waters of your own well to seek out the lost coins of wisdom? All kinds of programs can *look* good, and who am I to say they are not? I can only tell you that the power of one's program directly reflects the depth to which that program reaches. Do not be satisfied with the appearance of the surface.

On the other hand, beware of taking yourself *too* seriously. If you're not careful, you can spend the rest of your life investigating your belly button! As in everything, there is a balance. My own experience, however, is that we tend to avoid our wounded parts like the plague rather than risk going near them. Be assured that I'm not talking about spending the rest of your life justifying whatever gripe you may have about life's normal bumps and scratches. But I *am* saying that whatever deep part of you remains in tears will leak out into the present. This is true of every human being. It is especially important for *you* to understand, however. Why? Because not every human being is attempting to be healer. Not every human being would even consider grabbing the sparking ends of the downed power line.

The deepest form of self-care is seeing to one's own healing. Open your door and wait, my friend. Your guide will beckon you deeper into the mystery of who you are. It's way down there that you will find your new eyes—and your power!

Allow me to tell you an old story. I'll bet I haven't thought of this for nearly twenty years. But what did I know then? Just a little less than I do now, I guess. Anyway, when it came out of the dark and hovered by the fire, I was surprised. The truth of the story provided me with a jumping-off place farther down the road.

As I recall, David was a very no-nonsense, superrational kind of guy. If you couldn't count or measure something, he wasn't much interested in it. Then he hit his wall—or, you might say, fell down his rabbit hole. After a messy divorce he began to have anxiety attacks. Suddenly he was estranged from his kids, and he didn't have much of a life at all outside of his work.

David was always a "if it's broken let's fix it" kind of guy. He was downright offended by those anxiety attacks! Mostly, as he told me some time later, he *hated* the idea of not being in control. But when he felt an attack coming on, there was nothing he could do to arrest it. Willpower didn't work. Rationalizing didn't work. Hollering at others didn't work. Prodded by all this pressure, he sought help.

Eventually he found himself working with a lady who used a combination massage-nutrition-counseling approach in her healing practice. She was holistic before the word became fashionable.

David reported that after several months of basic relationship-building she led him through an exercise. She asked him to place his hand, palm outward, several inches from hers. "What do you feel?" she asked. "A kind of warmth," he answered, "probably due to body heat."

Then she led him through a quieting meditation and asked him to curl the fingers of his right hand inside of hers. Still in a meditative state, he was told to concentrate on the boundary between his fingers and hers. David could do this very well. He'd always been very clear about where he ended and someone else started.

Next the healer asked David to let the boundary melt and slowly allow their separate beings to merge. What she was calling for was a beginning stab at intimacy: the music of the Dance.

After a few moments, she asked David how he felt. "I felt nothing," he replied. "I couldn't even feel where our fingers were touching." But, he told me, he was slowly going emotionally dead. When she invited an even closer intimacy, he shut down as tight as the rock wall over Ali Baba's treasure cave.

Next the healer asked him to return his hand to its original position. Again their palms were held a few inches apart. Again she asked him what he felt. This time, with absolute certainty, he said he felt actual coldness—like ice. Notice that he didn't feel nothing or only an absence of heat, but actual coldness. By the time he told me this story he'd developed enough self-knowledge (healing) to know what had happened. Do you? Look once more at the Hoop.

Any genuine invitation to intimacy is the door to one's core. That's why David had backed off: he didn't feel safe. He had learned to shut down, not just in his emotions, but in his body as well. On some level his mind was in a panic that "it" was happening all over again: love being denied. His response was automatic: protect, defend, hide. Get out of the way at all costs.

The only thing that will hold you back is what you refuse to let go of.

❋

Don't flirt with the healing way as a lark, my friend. Why? There's a price to be paid. For one thing, you are going to be tried a thousand different ways.

Healing is about nothing so much as caring, and caring creates vulnerability. Nothing can hurt you if you if you don't care. But when you *do* care, when your heart opens to another, you become *reachable*. Beauty will astound and uplift you; beauty despoiled and wasted will crucify your soul.

Remember the old shaman and his magic fire? Now the smoke and shadows on my cave wall are conjuring up memories of a man named Perry and a girl called Star. Perry was a cop—a giant of a man with a face like a bulldog and the heart of a ballerina. That's a strange combination, I know, but there's no accounting for how life's cards get dealt.

For many years Perry worked the street. That all ended one night when he and his partner finally finished a high-speed chase by pinning the car of an armed thief against a brick wall. It happened that just as the robber slammed his car into reverse, Perry opened the door of his car to get out. The collision crushed Perry's leg. As the medics were carting him off he said he could hear the crowd hollering, "*Pig!* The pig got just what he deserved." Some of the onlookers were laughing, he said. The name-calling he could endure, but the laughing hurt worse than his crushed leg.

When that injury retired him from the street, the street was the loser. For all his size and fierce face, Perry was a lover. One of his great loves over the years was Star. That was her street name. She was a teenage, dope addict-seller of anything and everything she had—including, of course, herself. Over the years Perry must have known hundreds of Stars, but for some reason this one girl had totally captured his heart. It's like that sometimes. Who knows why? All of a sudden someone steps out of the crowd and unlocks a depth in you that you didn't know was there. Perhaps Star reminded Perry of a sister he never had or one of his own kids. Maybe Jung was right; maybe there is such a thing as the collective unconscious, a vast accumulation of all lived lives in a sort of reservoir we can tap into and that taps us. It might be that we all carry thousand-year-old memories. Maybe there was someone back in Perry's ancestry, someone he never knew, who was reaching out from the past into the present. Perhaps this still-vibrant soul was seeking to right an ancient wrong or to once again touch a face that had turned to dust long ago. Who knows? But, oh, how Perry loved Star!

More times than Perry could recall he'd look for her on his rounds. He always greeted her with a welcome, a kind word, a cup of coffee, a few dollars he hoped would go for food. Then Star began to fade. Perry would find her, pick her up, and carry her to a detox ward or hospital—anywhere she could receive care. I was with him on some of those rounds. When he left her, he would always tell whoever was in charge, "Take good care of her. She's a friend of mine." He wasn't threatening anyone, but I don't think any of the attendants missed his meaning.

The night Star died, Perry had found her unconscious in an alley. There wasn't anything left in her for life to hang on to. He picked her up and literally ran to the hospital. On the way everything in her failing body let go all over him. I don't think he ever noticed because it simply didn't matter. Nothing did but that core of beauty—perhaps that only he and Schemer could see—glowing beneath ugly names like "dope addict," "whore," or "loser" that hung like dirty rags over her true identity.

Perry was right there beside her when Star stepped away into the shadows. She just winked out. His grief was as great as her apparent loss. I didn't know that a man as tough as Perry could cry so many tears. She was a dried-up, emptied-out sack of a teenage girl. One of millions. *But Perry loved her.* She was special to him. If he hadn't cared he wouldn't have been hurt—but he also would have been a much-diminished man.

Perry had not failed. Life had failed. Star was but a single note in a much larger symphony that at that moment was swelling with sadness. If you allow yourself to love like Perry, you'll be tested every day, my friend. As clearly as your face in the mirror, you'll see that all around you a kind of sanctioned social cleansing is going on. Relentless forces seek to push aside anyone who is a chronic problem or inconvenience. Countless voices scream, "If you can't fit into our world, just live in the shadows—out of our sight and out of our minds. Rub out the disenfranchised, silence the messy problems of those who offend our senses. Be politically correct of course, do what is demanded, what looks good—but for Pete's sake don't let Star mess up your uniform. Be reasonable! The halt and lame are always with us, but you don't have to go out looking for them! *Stay out of the alleys.*"

I recall celebrating a long-ago Christmas at a party with some truly great people who ran a community drop-in center. No one had a dime. The party food was stale potato chips and soda pop. The music came from a resale record player, mostly broken. We had to tape a quarter to the arm holding the needle down to keep it from hopping around like a drunken jumping bean. I remember feeling so honored to be in such grand company. A voice from deep within me whispered, "This is the real stuff." You, too, will know when you are around what is genuine.

We got talking about Christmas wishes. Mary, the heart and soul of the operation—a clone to officer Perry, though they would never know each other—said with absolute certainty, "It's not just about money. We can get by without money. What I'd wish for is a busload of people who knew what they were doing. We can't really do much without the right people."

As right as right can be. Only healers heal. It's a matter of the heart, a question of vision. When you look at unkempt "nobodies" on the street, can you see their inner beauty or only the problems they cause?

Singing the healers' song is counterculture to say the least. You'll get off a few lines of your tune, and a hundred voices around you will groan in one way or another, "Oh, God, not that old song again!" It *is* an old song. A tired old song but no less true for being old and tired. Your inner band will strike up the march, and you'll jump on your mangy horse just like Don Quixote because that's who you are. You'll charge a thousand steel-tipped, twenty-foot long pikes that will tear holes in you. *But you won't charge alone.* I can't tell you what's true for you, only what's proven true for me. We must *earn* our souls every day, dear friend. Each day we make our decisions and we live by them. If you listen well enough, if you wait patiently enough before your open door and then go forward the best you know how, legions of angels will go with you. It isn't the kind of thing that can be proved—not by any yardstick currently in use. These days, of course, if techno-intelligence doesn't say something is so then it is dismissed as either trivial, fantasy, or a lie. Don't you believe it.

Such thin soup won't support life. Science knows not a damn thing about Perry and Star, nor about Schemer or the life beyond. The art of healing is of a realm other than science. Its values and perceived worth are wheels other than those used by society.

Unfortunately, the healing walk runs past schoolyards full of bullies. How quickly—or even if—you get up after a bully has knocked you down depends on the depth of your spirituality. Paradoxically enough, that depends on how well you have learned to take care of yourself. It took me a long time to learn that. When I started out, talk of self-care sounded like selfishness to me. Not so. Even though I've since learned the value of self-compassion, I still struggle with it on a daily basis. How does the saying go? If you would be another's angel, be first your own god. *You first.*

Perry's love for Star made her death especially painful. Why hadn't Schemer bailed her out? You, too, at times, will feel betrayed. A sadness as black as squid's ink will engulf you. Others' answers become your obstacles. Frustration abounds. You had better take care of yourself or your hurt will hurt someone else. Then *you* become the problem.

There is another piece here that wants your ear; I couldn't quite lay hand to it right away. I've been sitting here about twenty minutes, listening and waiting. Now I know—it's another thought about self-compassion. The urge we feel to move toward the light is rooted in the deep, inner impulse for self-compassion. It's the call of our own wounded self crying out for healing.

Have you studied the Hoop enough to know why this is so? Think about it. When the soul is denied its deepest need, self-compassion is the first and most grievously wounded victim.

When we lose (or never develop) self-love, witches of countless varieties are free to distort the mirror of self-recognition. The call is to self-compassion—whatever it takes to heal.

✳

By great good fortune I recently stumbled on a rerun of the old classic *Cool Hand Luke.* For lots of reasons I have a special love for that movie. One is that it was from a song Luke sang about "Good Old Plastic Jesus" that I got the title for the first book I ever wrote.

This time around one scene from the movie stood out. Luke is having a more or less running dialogue about God with George Kennedy, another convict. They talk about loving God and wonder if God cares for us. Paul Newman as Luke says that even if God does care, it is too late for him. He clearly believes he's on the other side of the glass, separated from God. In this scene he's sitting alone on his prison bunk singing the good old plastic Jesus song. The camera moves to a close-up of his face, a tear runs down his cheek, the words become slow and tormented. How many times have I seen that face and heard that expression of hope against all hope! "Despite what I think or believe, maybe, perhaps, in my deepest core, *despite all apparent evidence,* maybe, just possibly, there is a place for me in the light beyond. I'll be happy if you just let me sneak in the back door because I've never been comfortable with front doors anyway. Maybe if you really are Plastic Jesus or Mother Mary or whomever, I'll make it. I've never had much and never learned to trust. What I learned to do is hit first and take care of myself. You're better off if you need no one, ask for nothing. That's been my whole life; it isn't much. But if there is a place of light and peace up there, might there possibly be a spot for me? I don't expect it, but if it really exists, might a guy like me ever be let in?"

If you're looking for him, you will meet many Lukes. You'll see firsthand what trauma does, the trauma that is love denied. It strands a person at hurt and loss, stuck on the Hoop. It prevents intimacy. Those wounds stand in the way of that person ever experiencing the loving touch of God, of ever meeting Friend God. Hey, who *doesn't* sing Luke's song? It's all just a matter of degree.

❋

Just got out of the counseling office. Fascinating. Aaron is a really wonderful man, married with two teenage children. Now, for the first time in his life he has a chance to "strike it rich" in a business deal. He's been struggling along for twenty-five years as an insurance man. Somehow—well, he's sharp, that's how—he has figured out a new, highly profitable way for insurance companies to conduct business. He has heavyweight investors lined up, all ready to go. But . . .

Aaron's tree is bent! His terrible inner dialogue insists that he will never be *really* happy or satisfied. Why is he raining on his own parade? He grew up in darkness, and that inky, blinding environment has stayed with him.

As I said, he's a smart guy. Aaron realizes that even if he makes a success of his idea, unless important changes are made, he'll just be an isolated rich guy instead of an isolated poor guy. Aaron lives, as so many do, behind an invisible wall that keeps him in and others out. Love denied always builds walls.

Aaron loves his wife. She has stayed loyal to him for twenty-five years. She wants nothing more than to feel close to her husband. But just shy of "close" was exactly where Aaron learned to build his wall. He automatically shuts her out. Even when he *wants* to let her in, he can't.

The two of us hatched a plan to blast a hole in that lifelong wall. He is going to suggest a dialogue program to his wife. After all the years of hurt, I don't know if she can handle it. (Strangely, we want what most is also very often what we fear the most.) Chances are, even though she hungers for intimacy as much as he does, when Aaron starts to cross that line he drew in the sand, his wife will find herself pulling back. It's very hard to trust once your heart has been broken. Especially if that has happened day after day, year after year.

Do you see why I mention Aaron in this chapter? What about *your* invisible wall? Are you trapped inside, hungering to draw close to others but somehow you "just can't"? Do you substitute "doing for" in place of "being with"? Power is in being, not in doing. You must free yourself if you would help others find freedom. Tell me of your wall.

※

One of the worst things that can befall a person is to be successful at a lie.

What I mean by a lie is the coping technique we become accustomed to using, as comfortable as a well-worn trowel in our hand, to fend off the pain and fear of love denied. It's only natural to protect ourselves when we're in danger. But if we're going to walk the healing *way it's vitally important that we recognize what form of protection we learned early on.* Many people disconnect from feelings by escaping into their heads. Others throw themselves into work like crazed fanatics, or they prostitute their self-esteem for the sake of pseudoapproval from others. Sex, alcohol, food, whatever, can become our refuge. At first those techniques seem to work. The longer we practice them, however, the more a part of us they become. And as they sink deeper into the fabric of our being, they obliterate our view of all other options. Our defenses become our mind thinking, our heart feeling, our body sensing. We *become* the lie.

Even when times change and we no longer need the lies to survive, we can't let them go. They are us, functioning as our nerve endings.

At that point, those who would struggle around the Hoop toward home must begin the *unlearning* process by separating the lie from present reality and learning to distinguish the emotions sparking out of the heart of the lie. We must refuse to give them a seat at our table. The goal is not to despise those old friends—at one time they may well have saved our lives. The goal is rather to respect the wider view of *life as it can be* by letting the lies retire. Healing means walking in the light. To do that we must put down the swords we needed as children to fend off the dark. The more successful we have been with our lie of choice, however, the harder it is to let go of that trusted shield.

Mariette said it about as well as anyone could: "If you've been there, you know what these words mean. If you haven't, no words can take you there."

She was talking to her beloved family of suicide survivors. Mariette is one. At nineteen she found her father thrown away by his own hand. Today she was addressing a convention of perhaps a thousand suicide survivors. For a minute or more she looked out over the crowd, saying not a word. In silence she just stood there, in communion, sharing the Eucharist of the devastating experience that everyone in the room had experienced. The space between her and the crowd was pulsing with meaning. All the words in the world, she said, couldn't explain or tell them anything new. The silent affirmation of connectedness simply validated what had already been imprinted on each person's core. That validation bound them together.

You will experience many such moments, my friend. I pray you do. They are among life's most precious experiences. Deep speaking to deep.

Somehow in those moments of crystal clarity I always seem to sense a green light shimmering. At least that is what *my* dream factory conjures up. At times that light is as soft as a feather, at others as unyielding as steel. Sometimes it is intense enough to melt your very soul. Other times it is almost jolly, like a warm blanket snuggling everyone it touches. And sometimes it is downright hilarious.

Just yesterday a recovering cocaine addict went off on me about golf. As fiercely difficult as it was for him to clean up his drug use, he said that he never, *never* had done anything so difficult as deal with golf. Golf, he said, pitted him against his worst enemy: himself. He told me about hitting a three-iron shot perfectly. He said it was so sweet, such a pure experience, that he became addicted to the pursuit of a repeat experience. It never happened. But for seven straight months he chased that divine touch in the form of a little white ball with the passion and intensity only an addict can bring to the chase. (In case you don't know, addicts don't experience life the way nonaddicts do. That's why I can't really do justice to this piece of brilliant stand-up comedy.) To him, there was nothing funny about it. It was real. No games, no masks, no façades, no hidden agenda, no seeking others' approval or defying them just because they happened to be standing in front of you. It was real, right from the heart. Green light.

Remember Mariette's sense of not needing words at the convention? Well, quite near her sat another man, listening hard. When it was his turn to speak he opened his heart and told the crowd about his own father's suicide. His sister, fourteen years younger, had discovered the body. That was twenty years ago. Not until this last year had the sister become ready to deal with the tragedy. Healing is not about *living* in the past, but it is about *dealing* with the past. His sister, the man said, had been having a hell of a time. Major, fundamental foundation blocks of who she was had started sliding around. Doing business as usual was no longer working.

As the man spoke, the quality and tone of the green light between him and Mariette changed. A bomb could have exploded next door and her gaze would not have wavered. She was utterly cued in—not just to the words but rather to the person behind the words. She had been there. She *knew*. She understood that a healing program is a debt, not a gift. Someone was there for her, and by God she would be there in whatever way she could for someone else. Just like the man who showed up every week to start a new A.A. meeting, waiting all by himself, month after month, repaying a debt. So was Mariette. She knew of a group in the city where the man's sister lived. She offered to call her. I know Mariette; her voice will reach through a thousand miles of telephone wire to touch that frostbitten soul.

If you would heal, learn to see that light. Then make damn sure you're never far from its source. *No one does very well alone.* The journey is meant to be made with others. You must gather a team around yourself if you would escape being swallowed alive by the power of this interaction called healing. Go it alone too long, and you'll be as dynamic as a car with an empty gas tank.

By "team," I don't mean some buddies you "check in with" from time to time. I'm talking about the place where the green light glows. I'm talking about consistent, regular contact from the inside out with others who have been there, who *are* there because they've chosen to be there. Only they can understand what you're trying to do. Only they can tell you the truth, whether it's about opening up, turning aside, speaking up, shutting up, hurrying up, slowing down, or whatever. You simply must pull around yourself a number of those who would fire up their Comanche, just like Mariette was doing, and fly into the very mouth of hell if that is what needs doing. To stay alive and growing you need to tap into that depth and power just as a tree's roots need to tap into the earth.

You will have a million reasons not to. Too busy, too tired, unwilling to let others (nonprofessionals) see how hurt and needy you are. There are reasons without end. Your excuses may well be valid, *but none is sufficient.* Lacking roots, the tree withers and dies. So will you.

Find the green light and plant yourself there. It will nourish you. In real relationships you will find the real you. In this depth your own depth will be summoned forth. Somehow in this light, shimmering on the cave wall of your mind, God will reveal himself to you. And in a most amazing, mysterious way you will discover that the face of God is not a totally distinct reality from your own. There is blood in the relationship. In the image of God we are made; in our image is God known. There will be moments when it all fits and makes perfect sense. These glimpses beyond the veil come from the green light. So I urge you to find it and pitch your tent there. Plant your flag as far as you can reach into the light. Throw yourself into it. It will carry you, protect you, warm you, and always, always tell you the truth.

❈

A serious thought: As I said before, *most healers never get healed themselves.* That doesn't seem to make sense, does it? I mean, if healing is our business, then surely we should know enough to get the job done on ourselves. What kind of plumber would live with a house full of clogged pipes? Would it were that simple!

Maybe it is just the kind of people that some of us are. I find it so strange that many, many people seem *not* to be overwhelmed at the fire of life. Unlike me, lots of people I've met do not find it "just too much." Apparently (I have asked many people over the years), they're not visited by dancing shadows in the caves of their minds. Or, if they're visited, they're not aware of their visitors.

I sit here today, my friend, wondering who I am to tell you anything—I, who am so in need of healing myself! Strive as I might, the gift of self-compassion is all too rarely under my own Christmas tree. In my inner self, many of yesterday's bruises still tint today with a purplish black wash.

I pray that now, or someday, you understand that these pages are given to you as a gift. I know my poor dad wanted to gift me with his wisdom. To my regret, he passed on before I had the ears to hear. That missed connection is the sharpest grief of my life. Much of the passion in these lines is not only that you may know but also that he might continue to live.

These pages are as much gift to him as to you. His tree was so bent! As with every bent tree, his first casualty was self-compassion. I don't think he was capable of believing, of *accepting*, that he had a place at the table. He did what he could to protect himself and his response was characteristic of him. Rather than slinking off into the darkness, he charged the gate like a crazed Viking. His spirit was that of a raging warrior that never found rest on this side of the river. A raging warrior *never* puts down his sword.

But life cannot always be battle. If it is, your enemies are demons from yesterday as well as today. If there is no self-compassion in your life, you are running *from*, not *to*.

First, be a friend to *yourself*. As you fight ugliness, always remember that you belong with beauty. Paradoxically, only in your embrace of beauty will you find the legitimate strength to effectively oppose ugliness.

Life's dark side, if you are healer, will be a constant part of your spirit, of your vision. Like iron drawn to a magnet, your vision will be drawn to the hurt and suffering that many others dismiss or can't even see. You may not be comfortable watching newscasts or even movies or TV programs about appalling human suffering. For others it is just a movie, just a story. But for you, somehow, it is more. It is about people—bent trees weeping in the night. Those tears will flow through your veins like liquid fire. If you would be a healer, you will live with sadness. But how can you heal if you will not descend to the level of the wound?

You must also be able to accept the tenderness you extend to others. That too must be part of who you are. To a healer, giving is comfortable, if not effortless. Receiving is a very different matter. *Who do you allow to be your port in the storm?* Do you have someone you can count on to care for and protect you? As you journey ahead, you will stand guard over many fallen pilgrims until they can rise up again. But will you, *can you* accept that you need someone who will face the dogs of war and stand guard over you? Your work as a healer will teach you plenty about sucking it up and going the extra mile. But will you also let it teach you about seeking out healing solace for yourself? That, too, is a lesson that must be learned, my friend. If not, your soul will grow calloused. You'll be stranded on the other side of the river, trying to create bridges for others, marveling at the wonder of human balm, yet forever be a stranger to its magic. That's what happened to Moses. After leading the people to the promised land for forty years, he never crossed over himself.

Moses knew all about danger. Every healer is familiar with danger. But constant exposure to danger isn't healthy or normal. Tough talk about braving danger is all well and good. But we of the deformed tree have lived with danger for so long that we have lost, or never developed, a sense of safety. To us, personal safety is as foreign as moon dust on our shoes. Why? Because when danger becomes normal, safety becomes superfluous.

I've known many precious, powerful healers who give no thought at all to their own personal safety. They've set no boundaries around taking care of themselves. As much as they give to others, they give no thought at all to their own need for beauty, softness, or safety. It just never occurs to them. No matter how sick, how tired, no matter how outrageous the demands made on them, they never exercise the ability to say no. Does that sound noble to you? No, that's not virtue, my friend. More than anything, it's a sad echo of some version of love denied. No matter how much you do for others, if you can't deal yourself into the game, your own life is still screaming out for healing. You must be able to recognize the moment when it's time to put down your sword.

Spirituality is the source of all healing, and connection with God is the source of all spirituality. In that belief how can we possibly tap into the Love who is God if we ourselves don't experience his tender care? Your God wants you to have not just the power to charge dragons but also the infinitely deeper power to accept the reality of being loved. Not just loving. Loving is not that difficult. The really hard part, because of the bent tree, is accepting that *we* are loved. The challenge is not in stretching out a net to catch others when they fall, but to let go and fall into a net that's been stretched out for us. It is accepting that someone, anyone—let alone the One—would care enough to rescue us as we would rescue others.

You, too, belong, my friend. Believe that, as incredible as it may sound. Or maybe it doesn't sound incredible to you. I do not know the state of your tree. But never doubt that you also belong at the banquet. As much as anyone, you have also been called and given a place. "Physician, heal thyself" says the Good Book. Are you in need of healing, my friend? Where? From what? As softly and with as much love as you reach out to others, can you accept that loving touch yourself? Can you allow that beauty to touch you?

※

Words of longing, of trying, dated March 10, 1985:

> *All I hear*
> *as I search*
> *in the gloomy darkness*
> *year after year*
> *is a sure voice*
> *from somewhere*
> *somehow stronger than doubt*
> *where?*
> *promising*
> *dare I believe?*
> *I am here.*
> *where?*
> *not a maiden's first kiss*
> *am I lied to?*
> *but full of passion's fire*
> *could it be?*

> *as you have bled for others*
> *I bleed for you,*

as you have declared
and stepped forward
to take the first axe blow
I
declare for you.
I
step forward for you.
I
take the first blow.
You
cannot love more than I.

Little brother,
I hear you from the darkness.
Know I am here.
Put down
your heavy sword.
You have been exposed too long.
I am here.
Rest.
Let me
stand guard.
You are safe
with me.
I am bigger
than anyone else.
Your enemies are
within

more than without.
Allow me
to stand here
with you
against them all.

Dipping back into old journals. April 6, 1990:

If I let go
Will I rise up
or will I fall down?
If down
it will be to crash
upon the rocks of chaos,
this time perhaps never to rise.
But if I rise up,
coaxed by an insistent
inner voice,
I shall sprout wings
and pass like an eagle
outward
and inward
to the cool crystal spring
of hidden fiery ice
at my core
where lies my deepest wisdom
and the road
infallibly marked
to lead me home.

If only,
if only I let go.

I would know of God.
My voice said
         know first of faith.
I would know of faith.
My voice said
         know first of love.
I would know of love.
My voice said
         know first of self.
I would know of self.
My voice said
         know first of silence.
I would know of silence.
My voice said
         be silent.
I said, "I am afraid."
My voice said
         you have begun.

You
do not have to be strong.
You
do not have to be right.

You
do not have to be tough.
You
do not have to be good.
All
you have to be
is you.
All
you have to be
is here.
With me.
Allow me to be here
with you.
You have been
in the desperate land
alone and hard pressed
far too long.
Come home,
little brother,
it is time.
Let me
take care of you.
Let go.
I will do the rest.

Sometime I look at all this and tend to agree with what so many people have told me over the years: "God, Earnie, you are too darn intense. Lighten up! Life isn't all war. Every moment of every day isn't a life-or-death situation. Everything important isn't wading in blood or living in a gutter or behind prison walls."

Certainly, that's true. Yet each of us can only see life through the lens of who we are. What speaks to us speaks to us. I'm not telling you what is true—only what has proven to be true for me. For some reason I look around and see intensity even when it's wrapped in the greatest gentleness.

Mama Woody was usually a reserved, soft-spoken woman. But I saw steam rising from her great heart as she trudged into that meeting, just as there was a kind of terrible intensity in Jill's fragile clasp of Mama's coat. Perry was tough as a boot, but when he carried Star into the hospital he held her as tenderly as he would a bird with a broken wing. What could be sweeter than Sandy's prom? Yet somehow a very deep river flowed beneath the Platters as they sang their song. Monsignor Kern was gentle, soft-spoken, a slender stick of a man. He wasn't capable of violence in the usual meaning of the term. But when he approached his guest to share a smoke, his gesture harkened back to a knight on a mighty steed, lance point lowered, charging down into battle. Behind Gracie Rose's La La Lo, when she showed it to me, was a tiny little tear track running down her lovely cheek. Behind that velvet smooth tear were the howls and wails of anguished lost souls stranded on some dark continent. Danny, Old Blue, Annie—there is about their stories a dimension of incredible tenderness as they try to find their way. But somehow, coming from the same depth, is an intensity all its own. Maybe because it is all about love. That which we love we will hold most tenderly, but will also defend with tooth and claw.

＊

Purity—what guilty horrors, coming from my old-school Catholic background, surround that word! But let me give you another meaning.

Last evening Margaret, an old friend, called to ask if I'd address a session of her grief group. "We have no money," she said, "and we're few in number. But I believe the cause is important." How could I *not* agree to go? Let me tell you of that experience, my friend.

There were maybe twenty people there, average age about sixty-five. My friend was right—they had no money, no clout, no big name recognition. On her own, Margaret had simply gotten permission from several local churches to hold these meetings in their buildings. My bet was that she got permission but no real support. Margaret was "no one"—just a harmless, elderly widow trying to do some good where she saw opportunity.

That's *pure*, my friend. I was so moved. Right there was *the real thing*. This modest event and all the passion and energy behind it was not about popularity, glamour, recognition, numbers, scoring points, or making it big. This came out of real humility and selflessness. It was about simple, good people gathering together for no reason but to touch hearts and in that touching transform terrible hurt into sanctified humanity. It's healing at its best.

The evening after I had the privilege of sharing in this experience, I happened to be at a friend's housewarming. This friend is unquestionably a good man—a real seeker after enlightenment. But he also likes glitz. He likes bright lights and big numbers. That night he was telling me of a connection he'd made with the hottest spiritual guru around these days. In my friend's eyes, this spiritual teacher has "made it" by becoming nationally popular— and earning millions. In a very off-hand yet obviously proud manner my friend said, "He is the spiritual guide to the stars"— meaning movie stars.

Put these two people side by side. Study them. Let them soak into you. Become a shaker board over which these two realities flow. Can you draw out the flecks of gold that fall to the bottom? Let that gold fall into your heart, and it will be yours forever. I know nothing of this spiritual guru to the stars—let him do whatever he does. But I do know of Margaret and what she is about. God, how I pray for purity! And not only for myself but for you as well. To be pure, act pure.

❋

You've got to know where your angels are, my friend. You've got to be sure the golden ladder of love and beauty is readily available. Why? Because time and again you will have to find that ladder or sink.

I went to a hearing yesterday. It was a court case involving two lovely children, a boy, eight, and a girl, six, who were dependents of the county. The parents from whom they were taken claimed not to have the slightest idea what "this persecution of them" was about. The court-appointed psychiatrist read her report. She'd used a tried-and-true technique to help the little girl tell her about her life at home. She knew that children often project their experience onto their stuffed animals or make-believe people. In this case the little girl had told the psychiatrist a story about a family of animals. The little girl animal had to go to the bathroom. As she sat on the toilet she needed help, but the parents were talking to their friends. For a long, long time she sat there calling out for help, but no one seemed to hear her. No one came. Finally, the little girl animal fell into the toilet. Again she called out for help, but everyone was still too busy to notice. Finally, the daddy animal showed up. But after glancing into the toilet, he flushed her down "because he thought *she* was a piece of poop."

The psychiatrist's evaluation of the father started with the words, "His first and only concern is himself." The man was loudly indignant. He admitted to several "small mistakes," but certainly nothing that justified the removal of his daughter from their home. (One such small mistake was hacksawing the steering wheel off his wife's car because he thought she was seeing another man.)

Good and beauty are everywhere. But so are precious little boys and girls being flushed down the toilet. It fills your vision with such red-black clouds of pain and fury that you can hardly stand it. Beauty sprouts in abundance, but so do lost children. Consider the Hoop: What data is being fed to this little girl? What will be the foundation of the decisions that will dictate the quality of her life?

That's when and why you go to your angels—whoever and wherever and whatever they are. Shut out all the demands making claims on you. For the time being, you close the door on the knowledge that at this moment countless precious human beings are being shredded and there is nothing you can do about it. *Nothing.* You let it go, turn it over, allow it to drift off into the larger, wider tide of the Dance. It's time for you to find your golden ladder and rest there for a while. *You've got to have access to your angels.*

Many, many years ago a friend of mine and I adopted the word *esprit.* However the word is defined in the dictionary, to us it meant that sacred circle in time where you shut everything else out, open your heart as wide as possible, and let the healing power of love and beauty draw out the poison that threatens to close your eyes forever.

You can't make it without esprit. Find your angels, my friend. Keep them close. Never be too long removed from that sacred circle that folds you into the healing arms of beauty.

A quick, disquieting story: I stopped at a coffee shop to take a break the other day. Before long I was having some fun chatting with Rollo, the young guy working the counter. He was an especially engaging fellow, full of energy and enthusiasm. He wore his baseball cap tweaked off to one side, and he was half dancing to some rap music in the background. Outside the window I noticed a new, fire-engine-red Jaguar convertible sports car. It was a beautiful thing that must have cost a fortune. "You into cars?" I asked Rollo. "Take a look at that." He half danced, half walked over to the window to take a look. Seeing the car, he pointed to a man in his seventies sitting alone in a booth. "It's his ride," Rollo said. "Can you believe it?"

The man wore a gray silk suit that seemed to shimmer in the light. His long silver hair was sculpted into perfect form. He wore hand-stitched Italian loafers and a handsome gold watch. His clothes cost many a worker's whole monthly salary.

My knee-jerk thought was: when so many fight like dogs to make ends meet, it seems wrong for a guy to spend fifty or eighty thousand or whatever on a car. On the other hand, why not? That man has the right to spend his own money on anything he wants. If the car gives him pleasure and he is hurting no one else by getting it, then who am I to criticize?

Watching a split screen in my mind, though, I look at the hypercoiffed, silk-suited man on one side, and then see Mama on the other side, trudging up that dismal street wearing that ridiculous hat with holes cut out of the brim. Then she fades and is replaced by a succession of bruised babies born hooked on dope with nothing but trouble going for them now and a whole lot more in the future. The warring images grind.

But how far does a healthy person carry such thinking? Take it far enough and you could never do anything nice for yourself, even if it costs a dime! Where is the line?

At an informal rap session, officer Perry said that you can tell an awful lot about a person when you know what outrages him.

What outrages *you*, my friend? Tell me what outrages you, and I'll show you your values.

So I ask again: *What outrages you?* What grinds in your heart and mind like broken glass?

✳

Here I sit, thinking of a young man I know who recently committed suicide. This boy's pending funeral inspired me to finish this section with an excerpt from another journal I've been keeping for several years. I never knew my grandfathers well. One I knew not at all. I want my grandchildren to know their grandpa—they and any of their descendants who might give a damn. So I write to them. I tell them who I am and what the world today is like. I also describe the long-gone world of my boyhood. In fifty years they might enjoy reading it, like peeking down Alice's rabbit hole into a bygone time. So here is an excerpt from January 20, 1995. My wife and I were working and sightseeing in London at the time.

> We are on a train pulling out of Stratford-upon-Avon after visiting Billy Shakespeare's hometown. In two and a half hours we will chug into Paddington Station. It's very dark outside. This afternoon Grandma went to see one of Shakespeare's plays, while I walked around town and then visited the old graveyard to listen to the ghosts.
>
> How I wish you guys (my grandchildren) were here walking these ancient streets with me! If anything, Europe is about history, and history has but one basic, inescapable lesson: *you are here and then you are gone.* No matter how important you are, you have but a few short days, so to speak. Then, like the season's spent

grass, you dry up and blow away. So here's the question, kids: *did you make the most of your few days in the light?*

Who was bigger than the towering genius, Shakespeare? I stood at his grave. He was, is, just as dead as the no-name guy next to him. Did he enjoy the ride? Fifty-one years is all he had.

I stood in the National Gallery in London. I looked at the journals of Keats, Shelly, Byron—every one of them long since turned to dust. Each died in his early thirties. Famous now, but dead. Did they squeeze every drop of joy from their time on earth?

A London guide showed our group many narrow side streets just wide enough for two horse-drawn carts to pass. These little streets were built in the fourteenth century! You can still see the grooves worn by wagon wheels in the brick. Just ten yards away, modern London zooms about its business in ways those four-teenth century people would have called witchcraft! Yet I bet in their day those ancient Londoners walked beside their carts and talked about much the same things we talk of today as we dash about in our fuel-injected, high-speed cars: the weather, taxes, jobs, health, kids not respecting their elders. All the same. Who can doubt that six hundred years from now it will still be the same? So what mattered, after all was said and done? Did you get everything there was to be had out of your life?

When the tide of the Thames went out, we walked the exposed gravel bed and picked up tiny pieces of the past. A clay pipe from the 1640s, some chunks of green glass from a hundred years after that. Our guide said that he's even found Roman coins on occasion! People used them, made them, sold them, and then threw them away. Or lost them. If we could sit in a pub and listen to those people in their time (we did sit in what is left of Samuel Johnson's pub), the common thread would probably be much the same. Same conversation. Same gripes. Same B.S. Just like now. I look around, listen, talk to people (living and not) and ask myself, "What matters?" Nothing lasts, so what matters? Who is enjoying the ride and who isn't? That's about it.

My wife, Paula, has a distant relative, Roy, who lives here. He's the family historian of their clan. Before we headed home he took us some sixty miles outside London to an ancient little town called Wooten Basset. Paula's great-great-grandfather and grandmother are buried there. We stood at their graves. The old grandfather's name was Jacob. His son was James, who came to America alone when he was thirteen. That was shortly after the dawn of the nineteen century. James's son was also called Jacob, whose son was Joe, who is Paula's father.

Roy showed us a letter from James's time, around 1860, but it could have been written yesterday! James was very concerned about an uncle who was trying to get more than his fair share from a will. He went on and on about people we'd never heard of. No one remembers now that they ever passed this way. James was writing to a son who felt he was being cheated because he was working harder than a younger brother and was afraid he would not be suitably rewarded.

Nearly two thousand years earlier, Jesus used the same storyline about the prodigal son and his brother. If you remember, they had the same problem. This older brother was angry and indignant about his younger brother's laziness. Imagine all that emotion vented so long ago! Yet who cares now? Only that old letter was left to testify that the situation ever existed. Then James's time ran out. Did he get his due? In the final tally did it make much difference? What did it matter? Did he enjoy his short time here on earth?

This journal-as-time-machine comes to you with the wish that you enjoy your few days. Life is hard and the demons (fear, guilt, worry, grief, rage) that rob us of joy are many. God, how passionately I hope and pray that you avoid the worst of them! Achieve balance—that is the key. Never too much: for others—for self; work—play; have—give; strive—relax. Always strive for balance. The ancient Greeks had it right. *Arete*: excellence is in balance. Joy is not in besting others, but in mastering yourself. It is in living as freely as possible from the slavery imposed by your demons, in being motivated by the light, rather than driven by the whip of festering unmet needs.

The demons that rob us of light and ruin the ride are born in the bloody chaos of unmet needs. Basic needs. That is where things get thrown out of balance: bear down, hurry up, watch out, keep secrets, do more, do better, shut up, hide, don't try, attack, exaggerate to impress others. . . . An endless list of light-blockers.

Why oh why do we deny ourselves so much of the joy that is within our grasp? Day by month by year the sands are running out. Before we know it the book is closed and our time is up. Then *we* become the historical curiosity someone one hundred or five hundred years from now may wonder about.

Again, the essential question is: did we enjoy life? Did we live in the now or mortgage that precious sliver of time with worry and fear? Did we laugh much or miss those magical chances to tickle our soul because of anger or negativity? Did we celebrate often or waste those opportunities waiting for a "better time"?

But *now* is the only time we can be sure of. What *is* is the stuff of now. All those old, sad, failed messages of the bent-down tree will make what is seem not good enough. Tomorrow may be better. I hope it is, but now ain't bad. What is at hand *right now* is beautiful stuff. In fact, it's the celebration of joy that makes the ride worth the ticket.

This train is bouncing all over the place. I'm riding backward, my rear end is numb, I'm hungry . . . but do you know what? I am holding you in my heart and mind and your image glows like the sun. I hope you and all healers-to-be do decide to make a difference in the world, to leave it better than you found it. But be aware that many people who do a lot of good work never find much joy themselves. Many healers never got healed. What a pity! And how unnecessary! The crucifixion without Easter is just another senseless death. Good works are great, but joy is where it's at.

So here is what Grandpa will do: I will hold you and love you and pay attention to you and laugh with you and, together, we'll celebrate lots of adventures. In every way I know I will teach you balance. I will make for you the safest possible world so you will not internalize fear. I will be there always so you will not be wounded by abandonment. I will offer you my unconditional love—not only to spare you shame and guilt but also to give you a foundation upon which to build a powerful, loving image of God. I promise to offer you the kind of love that is given for its own sake so you never think you have to be other than you are—or can be—to be the recipient of the light. To the best of my ability I will affirm you enough that, for you, self-confidence becomes your reassuring guide through the swamp where the demons live.

A zillion other forces will tug at you. Ultimately you will make your own decisions about who you will be. But, by God, Grandpa will do his part to help you build a solid foundation.

This is what I wish you at the end of your days when your time has run out: whatever you may or may not have done, I pray that you will be able to say with shining faces, "My, my, what a glorious adventure!" Without that, no matter what else happens, you will not have been successful.

So there it is. I wish the same for you, my friend. Celebrate joy. If it is lacking in your life, figure out why and fix what is broken. Nearly any method will do; just pick what works for you, but get the job done. You deserve it. And so do all of you who are trying to help yourself and others journey around the Hoop.

chapter 7

So Strong Is Love

"THE FLAME WILL NOT DIE."

In a sense we've reached the end of the line now. But, of course, every ending is just the beginning of the next push ahead on the journey.

Just before I sat down to write this segment I heard Robin Leach introduce one of his *Lifestyles of the Rich and Famous* TV shows. One phrase he used was "fame and fortune, the final frontier." Ha! Not hardly. All healing is spiritual. How can fame and fortune be the final frontier if spirituality is both the quest and the guide? *Being found is the final frontier.* Returning home after being lost is. Discovering your true name is. That is the final frontier—the frontier of eternity.

These last words I write to you, my friend, are as much about healing as the first words were. Just as the wounding process has many levels, so does the healing process. I told you in the chapter "You First" that taking care of yourself also develops in stages. One level of the program is the constant, daily maintenance you must practice to stay in the Healing Way. And I've warned you that there will be times when you may almost totally disappear down the well of your hurt-self. Deep hurt. Deep healing.

Now, with all my heart, I tell you that there is an emergence into abundance. If you remain willing to face the darkness, there is a rounding of a corner from darkness into light that is as astonishingly beautiful as the hurt was paralyzing. Each of us will be led to a golden door within if we but follow. For all the fear and doubt, all the tears and sorrow, for all the torn flesh, there is—or can be—a healing. Just behind the door is a loving presence waiting to greet us, to whisper into our deepest nerve endings the hidden name that we've forgotten. In that moment we will discover that we are fully known—and that we will never again be deceived or taken advantage of.

Never again will we stand outside, alone, shivering in the cold while we watch others seemingly enjoying the community and warmth of good fellowship. For years, perhaps, we thought we had it all figured out: They, obviously, had already arrived because they had either committed no crime or already had been forgiven. We—equally obviously, but perhaps with no clear understanding of why—must have been outside paying for some crime we neither recognized nor understood. We were isolated because we were not welcome, not acceptable. The outcast's fear of approaching the golden light was greater than the pain.

I suspect for those who found entrance through that door into the golden light it was the first time they truly knew trust. At least trust on this level. For what really is trust but the discovery in fact, in reality, that *I no longer need my calloused layer of defense for I am no longer at war. I do not need to defend myself because I am not being attacked.*

The discovery that I am talking about, my friend, is an *experience*, not an intellectual construct. Experience is the only proof. Ultimately, only experience teaches. Thank of Rachel weeping for her children. Do you recognize the scriptural connection? Rachel was the mother of Ephraim in the Old Testament story. She cried not only for her dearly loved son but also for the whole people of Israel being led into slavery by the Assyrians. It wasn't just

Ephraim who was lost—it was the whole nation. Maybe that is what the image is really about—God's tears at humankind's creation of a world where countless children, of whatever age, are led off as slaves of darkness. Forever outside, standing in the freezing rain, banished from the party. If you look for it you can see Rachel's face in the paper every day. The faces of drought and pestilence, mothers of drive-by shooting victims, wasted faces of starvation and neglect pouring out of the African civil wars—all children who were meant to dance and sing, to trust and live without fear. All they asked for was bread; so many were given scorpions.

It is the journey of healing that leads people, one at a time, into the light of love. *So great is the power of redeeming love that no matter how long or grievous the hurt, a single act of unconditional love given by another can alter the course of that life.* So great is love.

To go out in the world as healer celebrates the strength and depth of the spirit in us, in our kind. Buried under the thickest rock, that spark seeking union with the eternal fire is fighting hard not to be quenched. The ache to return home is always there.

No matter how deep the damage, the strength of the spirit struggling to find its way to freedom is the essence of the greatest story in the history of our species. Every other accomplishment pales compared to the determination of the human spirit to embrace life fully. Bruised babies, children playing T-shirt catch over an institutional fence, Old Blue touched to his heart by the words of his ex-con partner Frank, tough, tough Gracie Rose softening up at even the mention of La La Lo, the tear of unspeakable grief rolling down the cheek of a tender boy named Danny who was ordered to murder every living thing he encountered in an Asian jungle and succeeded in mostly murdering himself—all having so much reason to quit, to simply die. Yet some part of them refused. The best part. The part that protects the flame with all the fierce passion of Thor swinging his mighty hammer. Or better yet the depth of the love that carried the Man hung on the cross all the way to the victory of his abandoned grave. What else is healing but the victory of life over death? God, too, refuses to let the flame die. He is the flame at the heart of the Hoop drawing all of us on our journey, mothlike, to its irresistible glow. There is our hope—our *only* hope as far as I can tell, my friend—for at the core of humanity burns a flame that hungers to be united with other flames in the Dance of Love. A flame that will not die.

There are shadows, to be sure. Life is full of darkness reaching out from the myriad of wounds on our collective soft bodies. All of these wounds are caused by love denied. Somehow we seem incapable of *not* inflicting these fearful wounds on one another; yet, at core, we all yearn for the same thing. We hunger for a common experience. All of us just want to get back home. Like the shaman creating his visions on the cave wall, we too cast visions on the wall of our own caves. Too powerful to be kept within, these visions use us to paint themselves by dipping their brush in the very essence of who we are. They go to our core, discover what is there, and then exercise their magic, their art. Peel back the thin surface layers of all the mighty commerce you see pushing and pulling all around you and that is what you will see. *Underneath it all is the song seeking a singer,* seeking to be sung by us. Afflicted as we are with human frailty and doubt, we sing the best we can but often badly, as people who only vaguely remember the words.

From the depths of my soul, my friend, I tell you that our deepest need is to respond in kind to the song that was sung to us so long ago. Our flame is but an echo of the love that calls to us in strange and mysterious ways. At odd times, whenever quiet wins out over buzzing activity, whenever our hearts can listen to the deep, we will hear the same, evocative siren song, calling us home. God has *always* been courting our souls. He has played the music just for us. He has spoken our names in a way only we can recognize. Sometimes we hear, sometimes not. Many of us have never heard that sweet sound, but still go on laboring up the hill in blind, hopeful faith. Perhaps what impels such noble warriors is the yearning for the shadow-love they never felt.

Every story is unique. Yet every story is so much the same. It's about the flame, always the flame. Whenever you feel lost or confused, just look to the flame. Both the direction and the answer are there.

Life is never about anything else.

Several years ago my thirty-one-year-old nephew died. Rich had fought a courageous battle for many years. I want to share with you a tribute I wrote about him. It takes our discussion of healing to a different level and ends there. You may not relate to the imagery. It doesn't matter. The point behind the word pictures is clear enough. *At the end we are led home.* When our time is up, we are fetched. It's all to the same place. The same direction. The same meaning. When the last word has been written and the pen runs dry of ink there will only be one line on the paper: so great is love.

Tribute from uncle Earnie

My heart is heavy! At 3:15 A.M. we got a call in London, and good news seldom comes calling in the middle of the night. The news was that Rich had traveled on about five in the morning on November 17. I swear the sweetest singers in the choir seem to be dying one voice at a time!

Rich is my nephew. (Even though he is on the other side now, he still is my nephew.) About eight years ago he had a wrestling injury and then was thrown from a mechanical bull in a club. The major vein in his right arm was badly damaged, leaving him crippled and in constant pain. If anyone ever lived nose to nose with life, it was Rich. To lose the use of his strong right arm was like an eagle losing a wing. A one-armed Rich was as unthinkable as a mighty eagle hopping around on the ground like a chicken. Unthinkable.

Attempting to bring back his arm, Rich underwent eight or nine major experimental surgeries over the years. None of them worked. Never would the eagle regain the use of his wing. Then, on November 17, Rich threw off a blood clot. It was his ticket home.

Sitting in Rich's room looking at the material remains of his life, my sister Carol (Rich's mother) told me what was sustaining her through all the pain. It was the look on Rich's face when she peeked in to see how he was on that going-home morning. He wasn't just sleeping—he had already traveled on. Carol said his face wore the sweetest, most peaceful look imaginable. A smile, really. That was not the face, she said, of someone who went somewhere he didn't want to go. It was the face of someone who was fetched. He was just *fetched* home, Carol said. Even the M.E. [medical examiner] who comes to all such deaths, Carol told me, took a look at Rich and said, "No foul play here. Look at his face; that's the face of someone who went gently."

Obviously, it's not possible to reduce anyone's life to a few pages of mere words. But let me tell you a bit about Rich so you can at least feel a glow, if not stand directly in his light. A story from antiquity jumped to mind when word reached me. Some four hundred years before Christ, the Celts invaded imperial Rome. They sacked the city for six months—and then left abruptly. The Celts were rural people, after all. They cared not a whit for cities or long-term conquest. As the story goes, a puzzled Roman asked a Celtic chief, "Then why did you take Rome at all?" The chieftain's simple answer was, "Because all things belong to the brave."

That's what I thought about Rich. He was brave. And more than anyone I've ever known, he experienced life. He did not wear life like a coat; rather he was the very thread that made up the coat. His was a unique gift of encounter, of *engagement*. There was just that in his personality that went to the core. He addressed people from his core, and they responded in kind. He was like a blind person who, for all the disadvantages of that difficult condition, was spared the misdirection that comes from surface masks. A blind person can't be tricked by the visual smoke screens we are so prone to present rather than risk rejection by revealing our true selves. That was Rich's bravery—he always went right to the core. His and others. For all the heartache and frustration of his injury and early exit, all who knew Rich were sure of one thing: *he lived*. Like a dog out for a walk that stops a million times to sniff, to take a look at, to explore, to enjoy what's going on *now*, so Rich lived. Therefore, all things in life were his, because he risked passionate encounter.

One of Rich's jobs along the way was as an orderly in a hospital. Being who Rich was, though, it wasn't really a job and he wasn't really an orderly. He simply had access to people in this place called a hospital. What he did was speak to their hearts. One of his favorite patients was a fatally ill old man who had played football for Wisconsin in 1922. Rich found this infinitely interesting. And the man was as proud as he could be of his former glories. He and Rich spent many an hour reliving those long past times, acting them out. Rich wasn't just humoring the old fellow—he was right there with him. The man had actually seen Red Grange play, Jim Thorpe, and Bronko Nagurski. Heroes! And he had seen them! Not as a clever technique but as a natural function of his character, Rich communicated enthusiasm that had the old man running for glory once again. In the magic of heart-to-heart encounter, young Rich and the old Badger were right there: it was fall, the leaves were falling, the stadium was full, and it was good to be alive.

Then one morning Rich went into the old man's room and found him in a near coma. With the genius that only someone who has been there could muster, Rich bent down and whispered in the old man's ear, "Once a Badger, always a Badger!" And with that farewell he gave the old man a golden ladder to climb from his bed and fly away.

All through high school Rich was on the wrestling team. Not tall, Rich was perfectly proportioned and immensely strong. There is a hold in wrestling called the guillotine. It calls for the executioner to roll his opponent over in such a way that a well-placed arm effectively cuts off blood flow through the carotid artery. As you can imagine, having your blood flow cut off tends to be a disadvantage. All through his wrestling career, Rich yearned to clamp the guillotine on someone. The problem was that this hold necessitates long arms to snake around the neck of your opponent. Rich did not have long arms.

But one fine match, Rich was pitted against a short but stocky wrestler. As the wrestling gods would have it, sure enough, Rich's big chance came. He rolled his opponent over just right, clamped on the dreaded hold, and watched the other boy start to wither—then Rich let him go. Like the Celts pulling out of Rome, he just let go. Later he told his mother, "You should have seen it. That kid was turning blue, a big vein was standing out on his forehead. He was starting to kind of twitch. I had to let him go. I couldn't keep doing that to a guy." That was just who he was. As tough as nails, but if you get inside the feelings of others as intensely as Rich did, well, he just couldn't let that guillotine fall to its conclusion.

He never judged. It just wasn't part of his internal job description to even think of judging. Rich was too much involved with the living, with the exploding *now* to have an interest in judgments about people. To Rich, life was a party that only a fool would miss out on. Who *wouldn't* want to mix it up with everybody there? A guy like Rich leaves a hole in many people's lives that simply will not be filled. They will go on, of course, but it just won't ever be the same.

Is God love? If so, it makes perfect sense to me that, when it is our time to cross over, we are sent a guide. Why not? I'd send a guide to someone I loved who was going into a strange place. In fact, Nell, a woman I knew some years ago who passed away at thirty-eight from cancer, told me that she awakened on one of her last days and there at the foot of her bed stood her two guides. She told me this as matter-of-factly as if she were talking about a shopping trip to Wal-Mart. They were two women she knew. Nell said that she flatly told them they would have to go without her just then. She said she still had a thing or two to arrange for her children before she could go. They left. But several days later she went with them.

I'll tell you what I think. I think/feel/believe/intuit that Rich had a guide. That is why he had such a lovely look on his face. And the shadows around me tell me who that guide was. Rich had a most complex and profound relationship with his grandpa, my father. They understood some truths about life deep in their hearts—things that pass way beyond the ability of words to describe. They just understood.

I know this sounds preposterous (you really had to have known him), but Grandpa was born out of his time. His century was the twelfth, not the twentieth. In all but culture, he was a Viking and proud of it. Even more than Rich, his clansman, he could not understand or tolerate all those empty suits whose primary skill is fitting in. Grandpa was as unique an individual as ever lived. He and Rich shared many a secret full of passion and sometimes dark magic.

What put that smile on Rich's face, I am certain, is seeing the billowing, fire-streaked clouds part in his final moment of clarity. Without a doubt he was watching Grandpa's dragon ship come gliding through, sails swelling, shield walls firmly locked, radiating confidence and power. Big Thor coming to collect his partner. That look of joy had to be the final fingerprint left by Rich's spirit as he went aboard that long ship and sailed off. I don't know what manner of Danegeld they collect in that realm, but you can bet those two Vikings are hard at it, loving every moment.

In that Valhalla there will never again be limitation or frustration, never again the vexation that comes from living among those who could never understand the visions that run and dance through the inner vault of a Viking's head and heart. Nowhere in that golden place is an arm that doesn't work or a back bent double in pain. Onward they sail in everlasting victory and laughter.

Our world is less for the passing, Valhalla the richer.

That is all I have to say, my friend.

About the Authors

Earnie Larsen is a pioneer in the field of recovery from addictive and unwanted behaviors, and the originator of the process known as Stage II recovery. He has written more than 60 books and 40 motivational self-help tapes. He lives in a suburb of Minneapolis, MN. Carol Larsen Hegarty is Earnie's sister and long-time collaborator. She lives in northern California.